S0-ASW-095

Writing from the Inner Self

Elaine Farris Hughes

HarperCollins*CollegePublishers*

Acquisitions Editor: Jane Kinney
Project Coordination and Text Design: Proof Positive/Farrowlyne Associates, Inc.
Cover Design: Kay Petronio
Production Manager: Kewal Sharma
Compositor: Proof Positive/Farrowlyne Associates, Inc.
Printer and Binder: R. R. Donnelley & Sons Company
Cover Printer: The Lehigh Press, Inc.

Credits:
Grateful acknowledgment is made for permission to reprint:

Lines from Stephen Sondheim's "Finishing the Hat" from *Sunday in the Park with George* © 1984. Reprinted by permission of Revelation Music Publishing Corp. & Rilting Music, Inc., A Tommy Valando Publication.

Shinkichi Takahashi's poem "Potato" published in *Leaping Poetry*, edited by Robert Bly, Boston: Beacon Press, 1972. Reprinted by permission of the translator, Harold P. Wright.

"An Appointment in Samarra" from *Sheppey* by W. Somerset Maugham. Copyright 1933 by W. Somerset Maugham. Used by permission of Doubleday, a division of Bantam Doubleday Dell Publishing Group, Inc.

Writing from the Inner Self, First Edition

The Library of Congress Cataloging-in-Publication Data
Hughes, Elaine.
    Writing from the inner self / Elaine Farris Hughes. — 1st ed.
      p. cm.
    Includes bibliographical references (p.) and index.
    ISBN 0-06-501437-5.
    1. English language—Rhetoric. I. Title.
PE1408.H6864 1994
808'.042—dc20   93-14406
                                                      CIP

93 94 95 96 9 8 7 6 5 4 3 2 1

For my students
Who inspired this book
and
For Stefanie Woodbridge

CONTENTS

PREFACE

All genuine writing begins with the self, with the moment when you dip into yourself—your memories, feelings, body sensations, observations, and imagination—and decide to bring something new into existence. Once you have discovered this continuous and fertile source within you, writing will become a never-ending, surprising adventure. New horizons await you: That is the promise of this book.

Writing from the Inner Self contains 48 exercises and about 300 writing ideas based on your experiences with the exercises. Each exercise employs some type of meditation or inner focus; all of them are designed to elicit original material from you. There are also several short chapters to help you with different aspects of your writing: using the exercises effectively, overcoming writer's block, keeping a journal, revising and expanding your pieces.

This book surprised me. I wrote it several years ago and thought I had said all that I had to say about writing from the inner self. Although that first book grew directly out of my classroom teaching, it was published as a trade book, meant for the general public rather than for college students. When it evolved into plans for a textbook version, I thought it'd be simply a matter of adding a little of this and cutting a little of that. I couldn't imagine what else I might find to say.

What happened, of course, is that I almost couldn't stop finding things to say. Prior to writing the textbook, I had developed the exercises as a way to generate in-class journal writing and there was seldom any connection between these writings and the expository essays students were required to write out in class. But once I began to incorporate writing-from-the-inner-self ideas regularly in my classes, ideas and techniques kept multiplying. With my students' responses and suggestions, I started finding ways to expand the personal writing generated by the exercises into more traditional expository essays required in college classrooms. All these new discoveries changed the original book into a totally different one—which is the one you are now using. My deepest hope for this book is that it will help you to love writing for the rest of your life.

Many silent contributors helped in the creation of *Writing from the Inner Self*. My major gratitude is to my students, who are the reason and the source for the book. Their pleasure in the exercises, their writings which have so often delighted me, their classroom responses, and their wise suggestions are the taproot of the book. Specifically, I want to thank the following students who allowed me to publish their writing in the appendix: *Darren Barje, Emilie Borg, Robert Bruck, Andrew Cohen, Cynthia Davis, Joe Dourigan, Robert Echeverria, John Falino, Karla Fitzgerald, Gregory Garry, Gregory Schweizer,* and *Robin Simkins.*

Any textbook owes a debt to the reviewers, but mine is a large one. The dedicated attention of the ten reviewers kept me going on what I often thought was an impossible task of keeping the original idea intact while tumbling it into many different shapes. *Steve Beck,* Southeastern Community College, North Carolina, *Susan Becker,* Illinois Central College, *Mark Reynolds,* Jefferson Davis Community College, Alabama, and *Charles Suhor,* The National Council of Teachers of English, all reviewed the book twice and offered strong expert advice on content and reorganization. *Judith Olson-Fallon,* Case Western Reserve University, *Nell Ann Pickett,* Hinds Community College, Mississippi, and *John Presley,* Lafayette College, Pennsylvania, and *Ben Wiley,* St. Petersburg Junior College, gave me encouragement and important suggestions. *Polly Marshall,* Hinds Community College, not only served as a reviewer in the final round but also tested in class many of the exercises in both books. To *Dick Graves* of Auburn University, I owe a special debt: His suggestions helped shape the present book significantly and his enthusiasm for the first book planted the seed which later became the textbook.

It's corny to say perhaps, but never truer, that without my editor, *Jane Kinney,* there would be no book. She believed in the book from the start and made it happen—and then kept me afloat during the rough times. I also want to thank *Lynn Miller* of Proof Positive/Farrowlyne Associates, Inc., whose calm expertise kept the production of the book on a steady course throughout, and my son, *James Hughes,* for his help at two crucial points.

Finally, I want to acknowledge several people who gave me ideas for specific exercises: *Arnold Bennett* for "A Throw-It-in-the-Fire Confession" in his book *Self and Self-Management; Dorothea Brande* for "A Five-Minute Concentration Exercise" in her book *Wake Up and Live; Aharon Remez* of Israel for "A Seven-Year Inventory"; *Ralph Nazareth,* my colleague at Nassau Community College, for "Sex Change"; and *The School of Practical Philosophy* for the centering exercise "The Pause."

Elaine Hughes
Nassau Community College
Garden City, New York
May 1993

The wine still waits in the cellars below.
My beloved family still sits on the porch in the dark.
The fire balloon still drifts and burns in the night sky of an
  as yet unburied summer.
Why and how?
Because I say it is so.

—Ray Bradbury
Preface, Dandelion Wine

Prologue: Bean Picking

You go out to the garden with a basket on your arm. Three people want beans for dinner. At first the pickings are so slim that you think you'll have to run out and buy beans or maybe just have carrots instead.

With each bean you pick, you think that this is the last one—there don't seem to be any others. Yet you keep finding another bean and then another. You're so busy looking and picking that you don't even notice the bottom of the basket, which is already covered with the long green pods.

When no more beans are in sight, you get down on your knees and search under the bushes. At first your eyes can't pick out the green beans nestled into the green leaves. But you stay with it. Soon your eyes grow accustomed to what they are looking for and you begin to find hidden treasures—many beans in clusters, others resting on the ground waiting for you.

Even so, moments come when you feel impatient with these tiny creatures playing hide-and-seek with you. Moments come when you feel that you're not going fast enough. There are many other things back in the house that need your attention. Picking these beans is interfering with your life.

But the beans don't understand that. They want to wait where they have ripened for your table until you can find them. They've done their job. Now they want you to do yours. So you keep picking. Some of them are not ripe yet. Others have decayed and have to be discarded. Some are so tiny that you think you should throw them away. But you need beans, so you toss them into your basket.

Finally, you've done all you can. You rise, look up at the sky, listen to the birds, take in the canvas of leaves above you, and breathe deeply. The hard part is over. You see that the basket overflows. Each little bean that you harvested has helped to fill it, and now there will be beans for three tonight at dinner. You make your way back to the kitchen, humming a little tune. Something in you remembers that this is how it always is. Yes, bean by bean—that's how everything gets done.

Part I

PRELIMINARIES

Chapter 1

—— YOU AND WRITING ——

Nobody else can write what you can write. You are one of a kind and have had one-of-a-kind experiences. On top of that, nobody else sees or feels exactly what you see and feel. If you're old enough to be reading this, you already have a limitless reservoir of thoughts, memories, ideas, facts, dreams, and fantasies from which you could write for the rest of your life. In fact, right this very minute, you've got enough material stored within you to write a shelfful of books.

The prospect of writing may delight or depress you. Or maybe you see writing as simply some activity you have to perform in order to get through a class. Perhaps you even hate the idea of writing or feel you're not a good writer or that writing is harder for you than for others. All of these feelings and attitudes are possible at different times. But whatever your particular situation or attitude is at this moment, this book can help you. The 48 writing exercises that follow lead you to look inside yourself first and discover a personal connection with the subject before you even begin to write. Stated another way: This book is a source book for using yourself as the primary source from which to write.

But don't expect writing to cost you nothing. Any kind of writing—good, bad, or indifferent—takes time, energy, and attention. Mrs. Lipsey, one of my most memorable teachers, said to our class one day when we were all groaning over the multitude of comments on our papers: "Don't you know that writing is harder work than digging ditches?" I thought that remark to be a playful exaggeration at the time; but since then I have come to know what she means. When you dig a ditch, you know exactly what is before you. The sun may be broiling, you may have a bum arm and indigestion, but you know that the ditch has to be four feet deep and three feet wide and you know that it has to be dug in six hours. You can see that it will require mostly physical labor and the determination to endure. The knowledge of those limits somehow helps you knuckle down and get the job done. But with writing, you never know what the limits will be. Writing requires *all* your resources—mental alertness, imagination, emotional response, a relationship with chaos, physical stamina, and the courage to face the critics who will read what you've written.

Yet, while writing can cost you a lot, it gives back far more than it takes. The very act of writing can integrate you in ways you may never consciously understand. In fact, I'll go far enough to say that the act of writing can change your life in positive ways. I've seen it happen many times in the classroom. For when you write from the inside, from the place within where the real you lives, you touch and transform many different aspects of yourself. Writing in this way is giving yourself the kind of close attention you've always wanted from others.

WHY MEDITATION CAN HELP YOUR WRITING

Down inside of you are many voices that want to be heard. As you walk around talking to others, balancing your checkbook, reading, and making phone calls, the voices murmur constantly; but they are sometimes low and delicate and hard to hear. There are also many memories and stories in you that want to be told. Under each of them lie layers of possibility. Each little fragment is tightly bunched with meanings—strands upon strands that can lead you in many different directions. But to get to these voices and these stories and form them into your creation, you first have to meet them down inside yourself. You have to travel down to get them. And meditation is the quickest way to travel there.

The way meditation works is all pretty scientific. Scientists made the discovery that our brain waves function at four different frequencies: *Beta, Alpha, Theta,* and *Delta.* Beta is the highest frequency and Delta the lowest. Most of our daily living is done in the Beta state—that state of mind when our brains are racing around at high speed. We get our business done but often at great cost to ourselves. Then we're saved at night when we spend regular time in Theta and Delta, sleeping and dreaming and repairing ourselves enough to face life again in the Beta lane.

But we're more interested here in the Alpha state, the frequency most often underused. In Alpha, brain waves oscillate at 8 to 12 cycles per second in contrast to 18 to 30 cycles in Beta. The Alpha state is the meditative state, that level of mind somewhere between waking and sleeping. We are awake, aware of our surroundings, but more tuned into our inner consciousness. This state of mind helps us relax and refuel our energies. We can solve our problems more easily, touch base with our intuitions, romp around in creative play. We all recognize this state, because suddenly everything seems just fine—we are breathing deeply and feeling in harmony with ourselves and the world. Bright ideas seem to pop out of nowhere into our heads.

So this is how it all fits in with writing: The Alpha state gives you a fertile place to write from and more to write about. When you slow down your brain waves and come into a state of relaxed attention, you become more aware of your inner self. At this level you will contact your most important memories and feelings as well as your most original ideas. From this source you can discover limitless possibilities for self-expression, for writing.

And you don't need to be leery or anxious about the idea of meditating. You won't be asked to do anything strenuous, dangerous, or uncomfortable. The meditations called for in this book are not that long inward journey into a state of nothingness often associated with meditation. The word "meditation" is used here as a term to cover a variety of inner-focusing techniques: conscious breathing, visualization, sensory awareness, guided imagery, and memory recall. All of the techniques called for in the exercises are short and directive and will help you approximate the meditative state quickly, with little effort on your part. All you have to bring is the willingness to be receptive to these techniques. Think of the meditations which accompany each exercise as mini-forays into your inner world—a place you can go to dip into your own reservoir of remarkable material whenever you like.

KEEPING A JOURNAL

And where do you deposit all of this remarkable writing material that comes forth? In your journal, of course. If you don't already keep one, now's the time to begin. Keeping a journal can turn you into a writer faster than anything else I can think of.

First, a journal keeps you in contact with yourself. It helps you put your thoughts and feelings into words on the spot, so you use writing as a way to discover what you think and feel. Immediately you produce writing with substance, writing that has a genuine voice with something to say. Second, a journal helps you develop many different writing styles. It gives you a chance to experiment in miniature with many different types of writing. Third, keeping a journal will free you up as a writer. It can knock a hole through almost any writer's block. Because you are writing in your journal for yourself and not some vague audience, you'll find yourself freer, more confident, and sometimes more outrageous and creative than when you're writing papers for others. Often you'll find that you can develop many of your journal entries into complete essays and stories, so your journal becomes a source book of ideas.

If you treat your journal as attentively and with as much appreciation as you do a good friend, it stands ready to serve as your audience, your therapist, your companion, your archivist, and your teacher. Eventually your journal will become a real person to you—someone you could not imagine living without.

Here are a few tips to be sure your journal makes it through the years:

- Use a good, stitched notebook, with or without lines. Glued-in pages and spirals don't hold up well.
- Write in permanent ink.
- Date each entry—give full date and day of the week.
- Start each entry on a new page. Don't cram your writing onto the pages. That way you can go back and add ideas if you want to.

In addition to using your journal with the writing exercises, you should begin writing in it on a regular basis on your own—at least three or four times a week. Make your journal a record of your inward journey, not just a day-to-day description of what you do. Don't treat your journal the way you did those old diaries you might have kept in grade school, in which you recorded every detail of the big weekend and every fight with your best friend. Your journal should be an *inner landscape*—a picture of how and where you are at a given time. You will be surprised at the pleasure you'll get when you go back and read your journal at a later date. If you need further inspiration for starting your own journal, look at the journals kept by writers such as Anaïs Nin, John Cheever, André Gide, Annie Dillard, May Sarton, Ben Franklin, Virginia Woolf, Thomas Merton, or Stephen Spender, to name only a few.

Most importantly: When you write in your journal, don't worry about correctness. Write as spontaneously and as honestly as you can. Let your thoughts and words flow freely. Write in your own voice—the one you normally talk in. Don't stop to censor your thoughts or find the "right" word or check your spelling. After you've written, *then* go back, proofread, and make corrections and adjustments until you're satisfied you've said exactly what you wanted to. Remember, this journal is for you. And it will reward you in countless ways.

SUGGESTIONS FOR JOURNAL ENTRIES

As a way to vary your journal entries and try out different modes of writing you might use some of the following suggestions. Don't forget to date your entries—one day you'll be glad you did.

Survey your accomplishments over the past six months.

Write down what you think about men (or women).

Put on a piece of instrumental music and let it lead and shape your writing.

Catalog every little thing that is right about you.

Respond to today's news.

Set down a bright idea you've carried around in your head for awhile.

Philosophize—about life in general or people in particular.

Write about the biggest challenge you now face.

Describe your favorite room.

Respond to a book, a movie, a record.

Take ten minutes to write out a solution to a current problem.

Record some unusual data you've collected.

Create a game plan for completing a current project.

Copy a favorite poem or passage of writing and interpret it.

Turn a page into a scrapbook to hold a picture, ticket stubs, a flower and write about its significance for you.

Analyze your most negative characteristic; praise your most positive one.

Speculate on where you'll be next year and what you'll be doing.

Fantasize about the big trip you're going to take one day.

Write what you think and feel about writing.

Recall an object that used to be important but has now disappeared.

Remember your most hated childhood foods.

Recollect an article of clothing you once loved.

List all your favorite songs or books from a particular year.

Do an inventory of the new things you've learned this year.

Compile a list of all your favorite short quotations.

Sit in front of a painting and write your thoughts and impressions.

Try your hand at writing a poem or song.

Speculate on the historical importance of today's date.

Describe your most romantic moment.

Tell a story about your long-ago neighbors.

Write an exact recipe of something you love to cook.

Write about a time you found yourself wondering: "What am I doing in this place?"

Relate a recent event which forced you to alter your established routine.

Explain an outdated idea which you think ought to be discarded.

Write a letter to someone and say what you can't say face-to-face.

A man and a woman are together on a train. Write what happens to them.

Give a capsule account of how you relate to each member of your immediate family.

Trace one particular color you've liked throughout your life.

Write a tribute to your favorite musician, actor, writer, athlete.

Shoot the moon: Write about what it means to you to be *alive*.

Chapter 2

THE EXERCISES: RESOURCES FOR YOUR WRITING

This is a book of exercises. But the word "exercise" is a little misleading. They are exercises in the sense that they will help you build your writer's muscles by giving you original material to write about and helping you to repeatedly exercise those muscles. But they go further than just the rote repetition we usually associate with physical exercises. They serve also as triggers that will release images, ideas, memories, and feelings in you. And they are also invitations which ask you to explore every aspect of yourself as the source for anything you write—whether personal journal entries for your own eyes only or essays that others will read.

HOW THE EXERCISES ARE ARRANGED

The exercises are grouped in such a way as to take you progressively deeper into yourself and your writing. They begin at the simplest, most concrete level—your body—and move into wider realms such as intense feelings, memories, self-awareness, observations, events, and imagination. They take you from the inner world to the outer world so that, still from your own inner perspective, you see the world in relationship to yourself. Each exercise contains some form of meditation, introspection, body awareness, observation, or a reliving of past events.

- There are 48 exercises arranged into three sections. Each of the 12 chapters contains four exercises.

  Part I: The Inner World contains 20 exercises on *The Body, Childhood Memories, Intense Emotions, Memorable Moments,* and *Observing Your Life.*

  Part II: The Outer World contains 16 exercises on *Seeing, People, Places,* and *Events.*

  Part III: The World of Invention contains 12 exercises on *Reading, Mind Play,* and *Imagination.*

- Each exercise ends with three sections of writing suggestions.

✍ SECTION ONE: *WRITING WARM-UP*

The writing suggestions in this section are brief and designed primarily to help you focus the experience—both the actual experience of the process of the exercise as well as the experience which you recreated during the exercise. Most of these writing suggestions call for a sentence or a brief paragraph, or sometimes a short journal entry. Occasionally you will be asked to describe how the process of the exercise affected you.

✍ SECTION TWO: *WRITING ABOUT THE EXPERIENCE*

The writing suggestions in this section take you further into the experience itself by asking you to write in more detail about the experience and to evaluate it in different ways. Most of the suggestions in this section can be used for longer journal entries or for turning a piece into a full-length personal-experience essay which uses narration—telling a story—as the primary method of development.

✍ SECTION THREE: *EXPANDING THE EXPERIENCE*

The writing suggestions in this section help you place your own personal experience into a larger context, to see it in relationship to the world and others. In these assignments you start with your own personal experience as the departure point and then significantly expand your thinking about it. Most of the writing ideas in this section will help you develop papers suitable for expository college essays or research papers.

How to use the exercises

Sometimes your teacher or a friend will guide you through the exercises. A number of the exercises really need another person to lead you through them, at least the first time. But many times you will be doing them on your own and will soon become proficient in doing them alone. When you use the exercises independently, read through them ahead of time so you are familiar enough with them to close your eyes intermittently as you go through the process. You might even consider tape-recording some of the exercises in your own voice and playing them back to yourself while you close your eyes. The exercises are all brief and can be read aloud in a few minutes. The meditation process in most of the exercises averages around six to eight steps and takes between three to seven minutes to complete before the writing begins.

Here are a few guidelines for getting the most from the process of the exercises whether doing them on your own or being guided through them by someone else:

- *Keep Your Eyes Closed During the Exercise*
  Keeping your eyes closed during the process will increase the vividness of your inner eye and will intensify your concentration. If you are doing the exercise on your own, open your eyes only to read the directions; otherwise, keep them closed.
- *Begin Writing as Quickly as Possible*
  As soon as you finish the process and have had a moment to reflect, begin to write as quickly as possible without stopping to think or take a break. In other words, write before any of the material evaporates.
- *In the Beginning, Forget Correctness*
  Don't stop to go back and read what you've written until you've finished. Forget correctness until later, don't struggle for the "best" word, and don't try to be a "good" writer. The most important challenge for you is to be as honest and as specific as possible.
- *Don't Stop Writing Too Soon*
  Push yourself to keep going, even when you feel as if you've written enough. Sometimes the most important material emerges at the end, so keep writing until you discover something significant for yourself.

Some of the exercises might suit you exactly; others might not attract you a bit. But stay open to all of them. Think of them as a smorgasbord and take a little taste of each of them at least once. You might want to do some of your favorites more than once and thus yield new layers of exciting material. Open yourself to surprise. Have fun reclaiming all those shiny bits of information about yourself. And, above all, never use any of the material you get from these exercises as a weapon with which to threaten or condemn yourself. Greet whatever emerges as heartily as you would a long-lost friend.

FOUR MEDITATION TECHNIQUES WITH WRITING WARM-UPS

Most of the exercises ask you to inwardly focus before beginning, such as by paying attention to your breathing, tuning into your body, or visualizing a scene. There are four basic techniques that you'll be using in the exercises:

- Centering: The Pause
- Spiral Breathing
- Visualizing
- Memory Recall

The four techniques, which are explained below, step-by-step, progress in length and complexity. All of them are easy to learn and use. After each of the

niques you'll find a few warm-ups which ask for a brief journal entry. rm-ups will help you make the transition from inner focus to out-
...ning and will prepare you for the longer exercises that follow. Try each of them on your own or have your teacher or a friend read them to you.

CENTERING: THE PAUSE

During a short pause of one to three minutes, you will focus your attention and become centered in your body. It's a good idea to begin every exercise with the pause, but it is an especially important technique to use for those exercises that are done with your eyes open. You can use the pause throughout the day to focus your attention; it's also effective if you use it immediately before beginning any activity.

Sit up straight, hands on thighs, with your back away from the chair.

Fix your gaze on a spot on the floor. (Keep your eyes open throughout.)

Become aware of your body.

Still keeping your gaze fixed, become aware of things on either side of you.

Become aware of how your feet feel on the floor, how your clothes feel against your skin, and how the air feels as it circulates around you.

Extend your hearing to the farthest sound. Allow every sound to come into your hearing and then recede.

Keep your gaze fixed and your attention focused until you feel calm and centered.

Take several deep breaths and then begin writing.

━━━━■━━━━

✍ WRITING WARM-UP

Write down a catalogue of all the sounds that reached your ears while you were in the pause. Next describe what you saw while your gaze was focused. End by explaining how you felt as you sat through the pause.

SPIRAL BREATHING

There are numerous breathing techniques that will help you concentrate on your breathing and thus relax you mentally and physically. Here's one you can learn and use regularly before beginning the exercises.

Sit up straight, feet firmly on the ground, with your back away from the chair.

Begin by simply observing your breathing. Don't judge it or make any attempt to adjust it. Simply breathe and observe.

Next, to the count of seven, imagine that your spine is like a thermometer with a red ball at the base. Breathe deeply and pull the red ball up through your spine. Imagine it circling slowly and traveling all the way to the top of your head.

Hold your breath and see it circling several times around your head. Exhale slowly to the count of seven and imagine the red ball dropping gently back to the base of your spine as your breath circles back down.

Exhale fully allowing your lungs to empty completely. Let a few seconds elapse in which you are not breathing at all. Then expand your lungs and take in another deep breath and repeat the exercise. Each time you repeat the process, allow your body and mind to relax and let go more and more.

———————■———————

✎ WRITING WARM-UP

Explain what you discovered about how you breathe. Did you notice anything unusual about either your inhalation or your exhalation? Include how you felt after the exercise.

VISUALIZING

Visualizing is an important part of nearly all the exercises. It is simply the art of tuning into the movie in your head—and your head is constantly making a movie. During the majority of exercises, you will be asked to close your eyes and imagine an object, a person, or a scene. When you visualize, you actually *see* pictures on your mental screen and, with your eyes closed, you usually see these mental pictures vividly. Here's a simple technique to help you start visualizing:

Close your eyes and imagine a large TV screen in front of you.

Project a red rose onto the screen and look at it for a few moments.

Now change the red rose to a purple one.

Then change the purple rose to a yellow one.

You've just visualized—it's that easy. You can practice doing this with other objects such as a coat, an automobile, an umbrella, or a puppy.

Once you've mastered simple visualization, you can gain further practice by doing the following:

Close your eyes and imagine yourself in a beautiful place in nature. See the time of day, the season, and your surroundings. Watch yourself walking slowly through the lovely setting. Observe all the different things you pass as you walk.

Now stop and sit down. Notice what you have chosen to sit close to. Look around and observe what you see from this new vantage point.

Suddenly some activity happens far away from you, but you can observe it from where you sit. Watch what happens closely, paying attention to the sights and sounds that occur.

After the action is over, see yourself getting up and walking back the way you came. Notice if anything has changed in the setting as you return.

———————■———————

✍ WRITING WARM-UP

Write down any scene or piece of scene that you remember seeing. Focus on the one thing that was most vivid for you. Then assess how well you were able to visualize.

✍ WRITING WARM-UP

Close your eyes and visualize a sweater that you own. Look at the material closely. Notice if there are any patterns. What is the color of the sweater? Change the sweater in some way. Open your eyes and describe the sweater in detail and then explain how it looked after you changed it.

✍ WRITING WARM-UP

Close your eyes and visualize a scene from a movie you remember seeing. Really see the scene from beginning to end. Slow down the action so that you can examine all the details: who the people are, what they are wearing, what they are doing, and what they are saying. Look at the surroundings. Notice any unusual objects. Now open your eyes and write down the scene in as much detail as possible.

MEMORY RECALL

Many of the exercises in the book ask you to remember people, events, or feelings that you have experienced in the past. Gaining access to your past will give you vast amounts of material from which to write. You can use the following exercise when you want to go very deep into your memory and retrieve buried information.

Close your eyes and relax yourself with several deep breaths.

Imagine yourself going inward and then far down. You can do this by imagining yourself
curling into a soft ball, which bounces down stairs into the basement; or being on an elevator, descending toward a dimly lit lower floor (and you can count down the floors as you go); or free-falling into a warm, safe darkness and landing on a soft bed of feathers or grass.

Once you are at a deeper level of feeling and thinking, call forth a picture of yourself at any age. Just think of any age, see what comes up, and take whatever it is.

Stay with yourself at this age for a few minutes and try to recapture how you looked and felt at that time in your life. It will help to remember where you lived and who your friends were at the time, what you wore and the things you liked to do.

Now allow any scene from that age to appear in front of your mind's eye. Look at what is happening very closely. Tune in to all your senses—what you see, hear, smell, taste, and feel. Stay with it until you get the feeling that the moment is actually happening all over again.

Let the scene dissolve and imagine yourself rising back to the surface, back up to reality. You can do this to a slow count of ten. When you come out of the regression, take time to recall all you experienced.

———■———

✍ WRITING WARM-UP

Write about yourself at the age you saw yourself most vividly in the exercise. What were you like then? What were your most important desires? After you've written a general summary of yourself at a certain age, describe in detail the scene you saw and speculate on why it still matters to you.

✍ WRITING WARM-UP

With your eyes closed, recall everything you can about yesterday. How did you start your day? What were the major events? How did you feel at different points? How did you end your day? Open your eyes and write down everything you recalled.

✒ WRITING WARM-UP

Remember an important party that you attended last year or the year before. Close your eyes and put yourself into the middle of it. Observe your surroundings and the other people. Who is with you? See yourself as you looked then. Observe in detail how you dressed and looked and acted. Write an account of the evening.

✒ WRITING WARM-UP

Remember how you wore your hair at some point in grade school—the third, fourth, fifth, or sixth grade, for example. Close your eyes and go back to that time and really see yourself. Look closely at your hair. Who styled your hair back then? How did you feel about your hair? How did you wear it? What color was it? Open your eyes and write a short piece about your hair back then.

Chapter 3

GETTING WORDS ON PAPER

You probably already know from experience that writing doesn't happen in an organized, straight-to-the-point way. Writing is chaotic—especially the first draft—and learning to like, even to welcome, this chaos is part of becoming a happy writer.

Nevertheless, beyond the creative chaos lies a fairly predictable process for producing a finished paper. Once you have generated a piece of writing that pleases you, you can take steps to turn it into a paper that others enjoy. In fact, there is a specific process for doing so. Here it is, step by step.

WRITING PAPERS USING THIS BOOK: THE PROCESS

Generating Content

The first step in any writing process is to generate content. Ideally, the content for your writing should be uniquely yours. And that's where using the exercises comes in.

- Put yourself into a receptive state. Do the pause and/or spiral breathing before beginning.
- Do one of the exercises—either on your own or have someone guide you through it.
- After the exercise, begin writing rapidly without censoring yourself. Use one of the writing suggestions in the Writing Warm-up or Writing About the Experience sections that follow each exercise. If you get stuck, return to useful steps in the exercise.

Shaping the Writing

After you've generated a piece of writing that you like, you can take it further and begin to turn it into a paper that others might read.

- At this point, either use one of the writing suggestions in the Expanding the Experience section or develop the piece you have written into a fuller paper.
- After this step (or before it, if you are stuck), read what you've written aloud to a friend or group of friends. Talking to others about what you've written and getting their responses will give you many new ideas for expanding the paper further.

Note: Following this section are guidelines for reading aloud and for responding to other peoples' papers.

Creating a Full Draft

Using the ideas friends or classmates gave you, think now about producing a full-length, polished paper.

- Go through what you've written and make notes where you will need to add information and where you will need to cut. Then rewrite your paper until it seems complete to you.
- At the end of your first full draft, write one sentence that expresses the major point you want to make. Put that sentence on an index card and keep it in front of you.
- Now is the time to gather additional information if you need it. This research might include reading, talking to or interviewing others, watching films, doing general research of any kind, or redoing parts of the exercise to retrieve additional details.
- Expect to write a second and a third draft. Don't be lazy about writing several drafts. This step will be essential in helping you clarify your ideas. Through this process, you will reach a somewhat natural organization for your paper. If not, list all the ideas in your paper and outline them to keep you on track. If that doesn't work, get some help from a friend or your teacher. Sometimes another eye can see clearly the shape a paper wants to take.
- Once you're satisfied with content, go through and read your paper aloud once or twice. Listen closely for how the paper really sounds. Rewrite awkward sentences. Make corrections. Add necessary transitions for smoothness. Fill in missing details for clarity. Pare down spots that drag. Then read this draft to a friend if possible.

Producing a Final Paper

Now comes the final product, the paper that should sound as if you're an expert on your subject and that you just tossed off the paper in a few hours. It should sound effortless to your reader, of course—but it won't, unless you do some important behind-the-scenes work.

- Type a full draft. Use a word processor if possible to simplify additional editing.
- Read your paper aloud again and clear up any awkward or sluggish spots. Edit closely for correctness in spelling, verb usage, agreement, and other grammar problems that crop up for most writers.
- Now you're ready for the final copy. If you're using a word processor, run the paper through the spelling checker to catch errors you might have missed. Next proofread slowly on the screen, paying attention to page breaks, formatting, omitted or repeated materials, and other possible glitches.
- After you have a printed copy, proofread it closely two or three times. Slow down and look for errors. Expect them; all papers have them. Make corrections neatly in ink. And there you have it—a piece of your very best self to show off in public.

The final section of the book, Part V, will give you more detailed help in expanding your early drafts and in polishing your final revisions.

YOUR WRITING PROCESS

No two people write alike. The way you compose a paper will be different from anybody else's. What will be useful to you as a writer is to keep up from time to time with how you created a piece of writing. Before long you will gain more understanding of how you work as a writer and can begin to use your writing process consciously, capitalizing on your strengths and tolerating your weaknesses.

Analyzing your writing process is fairly simple; here are two ways:

Immediately after you've written a piece, write a short paragraph under the general heading of "How I wrote what I wrote." Talk to yourself on paper and remind yourself of the different stages you went through as you wrote. If you are working on a longer piece over the course of several days or weeks, take time to write a few paragraphs about how you're working at different intervals. These brief writings will make you very conscious of your composing process.

When you're writing a first draft or writing informally in your journal, you can use the split-page technique. Draw a line down the middle of a page. Write your content on the left side and keep a running commentary on the right—observe yourself, argue with yourself, jot down all the subterranean ideas that occur to you while you're in the process of composing. This technique yields insights as well as new ideas.

READING YOUR PAPERS ALOUD TO OTHERS

The thought of reading your writing aloud might scare you at first. However, reading your work aloud goes hand in hand with your development as a writer: It will help you develop a strong writing voice and sharing what you have to say with others will give you a feeling of satisfaction. Most writing classes devote some time to reading aloud, or you can pair up with other students or friends and listen to each other's work out of class. Here are a few tips to help the process along:

When You Read Aloud

Slow Down. Read much slower than you talk. Your listeners will not be able to follow you if you read at the same speed you use in conversation.

Turn Up the Volume. Read in a loud voice—much louder than when you ordinarily talk. Make sure your voice carries to each listener.

Add Drama. Call forth the actor in you. Make what you've written demand to be heard.

Don't Verbally Explain Your Paper. After you have read, listen closely to comments and questions, but don't spend time explaining your paper. Use your time to consider which responses are valuable. Save your ideas and energy for the next draft.

Make Notes for Future Revision. Make notes at spots that you may later want to rewrite or expand. If your listeners asked questions or gave you ideas, jot down those that seem important to you. As you read, you probably noticed spots that didn't read exactly as you thought they would. Make notes there also.

When You Listen to Others Read

Relax and Open Up Your Hearing. Don't struggle to listen. Just stay in the present and focus your attention on the sound of the voice that is reading. Rather than trying to remember everything you hear, simply notice what you do actually hear and remember.

Don't Interrupt. Save your questions or comments until the end. Make notes of anything you want to remember. Don't distract the writer in any way while he or she is reading.

Respond to the Writing Simply and Honestly. Rather than trying to find something nice to say or making general remarks such as, ''That's really good,'' which aren't helpful to the writer at all, organize your comments around these two ideas:

What I Heard. Which details do you easily remember? Give the writer back his or her words. Say what stood out for you. These details are important because the writer then knows these are strong parts.

What Was Missing for Me. Where were the gaps? Tell the writer what you wanted to know more about, and which details would make the writing more complete for you. Point out anything that wasn't clear to you. This information helps the writer see the spots that need expanding.

KEEPING THE FLOW OF WRITING GOING

As you move into the exercises in this book and begin to write out of your experiences with them, you will find that writing will become easier and easier for you. Still, there may be times when you get stuck or when you feel uninspired and have nothing to say. Sometimes, no matter what you do, you might come up against that brick wall—the well-known writer's block. This block might especially happen when you have to write on command to meet an assignment or deadline. At these times, a couple of techniques can come to the rescue—and you can return to these techniques and tips at any point when you hit a snag. They'll be here waiting for you.

Freewriting

You may already know that the quickest remedy for writer's block is to write. And you may already know something about *freewriting*—writing as rapidly as possible so that you will write through any resistances you might have. You can use freewriting to discover many things: what you think, how you feel, what you know, and even what kind of structure a particular piece of writing seeks. Freewriting requires only that you sit yourself down and do it. Have faith that words will come to you. The truth is that there are thousands of words and ideas that belong only to you and come to you every day. And freewriting is a proven method to help you spill out some of those thousands of words rattling around in your head.

Freewriting can be either *unfocused,* in which you record random thoughts as they occur, or *focused,* in which you write with a definite subject in mind. You use unfocused freewriting, for example, when you pick up your journal and write without thinking at all what you will say. When you use the writing suggestions following the exercises, you will be using focused freewriting because you will have a subject in mind as you write. If you are required to write about a certain subject, you can often use focused freewriting to discover what you know and think about the subject and thus find a center point from which to write your paper.

Here are some basic techniques for freewriting. They are the same whether the freewriting is focused or unfocused.

Freewriting Techniques

- Get comfortable. Put yourself into a situation that will help you sink into the writing. Take a moment to do the spiral breathing or the pause.
- Put a clock or watch nearby. A timer also works well.
- Decide on a firm amount of time for writing and don't stop until the time is up. Ten to 20 minutes is a good block of time for freewriting, but sometimes even two or three minutes can yield an exciting result.
- Use a pen and notebook (use your journal if you like) or compose on a word processor or typewriter if you prefer.
- Now start writing as fast as you can. Begin with whatever ideas pop into your head. Don't stop except to breathe or turn the page. At first you may feel stuck. If so, write the word "stuck" or a bland word such as "and" or "it" over and over until more words come.
- Don't stop to think or to correct yourself; don't pause to search for the best word. Don't worry about punctuation or spelling. Trust yourself. Just plow on through with the knowledge that you'll come back to it later.
- Give your inner critic a sleeping pill. For at least these few minutes, turn off any judgments about what's coming out of you in the freewriting. No matter how strange or disjointed it may seem, let it rip. In spite of what your critic says, you *can* write—and are entitled to do so.
- When the time's up, quickly read what you've written, add anything else you want to, or make notes about what you want to add later. Then put it away for awhile. This is not the time to begin serious editing.

Whenever you feel stuck on any project, turn to freewriting. A couple of freewrites will nearly always get your adrenalin going and will usually produce bright ideas which you can actually use.

But just in case you need a little extra shove through writer's block from time to time, there follow a couple of idea-generators: A List of Lists and Ten Tips for Writer's Block. Keep in mind that behind your toughest blocks, you will often find your best material. And the exercises in the rest of this book will help you push through those blocks and lead you to your own gold mine of irresistible material.

A LIST OF LISTS

A quick and easy remedy for writer's block is to make lists. This technique is especially good for those days when you can't get even six words together for a freewrite.

Choose a topic from the following group (or make up your own) and rapidly make a random list. Set the clock for ten to 15 minutes and don't stop until time's up. Keep at it even though you feel you've exhausted your brain. Push yourself to make a *long* list. Some of the words that tumble out uncensored might spark you into actual writing. And, if not, at least you now have a list of potential writing ideas.

Major Irritations

Good Things About My Writing

Ways I'm Unkind to Myself

Unusual Experiences I Have Had

The Different Masks I Wear

All the Things That I Like About Myself

Old Yearnings

New Ambitions

All the Things I What That Money Can't (or Can) Buy

Physical Ailments That Plague Me

Pets I Have Loved

Pieces I Want Someday to Write

People I Miss

Childhood Delights

Some Gratitudes

Sensuous Pleasures

Ideas That Intrigue Me

Unusual Things That Have Happened to Me

Objects I Have Loved

Secrets

Favorite Books (Songs, Plays, Movies)

Old Ideas That Ought to Be Discarded

Things My Grandparents Probably Knew

Things I Know How to Do

Information I Would Like to Have

TEN WRITING TIPS FOR WRITER'S BLOCK

Write about what you would write about if only you didn't feel blocked.

Write about what you will—at some future point—actually write about. (You can start with a list and expand it with descriptions at a later date.)

Write about your ideal game plan for completing a writing project. (Maybe, "I'll feel over the hump when I have. . . ." Follow with a list.)

Write the smallest possible segment of a larger piece. Instead of a whole story or even a paragraph, concentrate on an opening sentence or a 100-word description of someone's hat. Working in miniature can often warm your creative juices to more writing.

Write a list of subjects you *want* to write about one of these days.

Write down what you think you can accomplish on your writing goal or project *for today only*. Don't think beyond today, and force yourself to put down less than you think you can do.

Write down what you overhear other people say. Steal lines while you're in a café or on a bus. You'll be amazed at how lyrical some of it is. You can arrange all the lines into a poem or write some dialogue. At any rate, this tip will at least get you out of the house.

Write for seven (*only seven*) minutes. Set a timer or an alarm and, when it rings, force yourself to stop. If you're miserable in your writing, then you're saved. If you're ecstatic in your writing, so much the better. By having to quit, you'll be panting to get back soon.

Write in detail about every single thing you did yesterday. (Did you do any writing of any kind? Give yourself credit if you did.)

Write a log of every minute you spend each day on *any* writing. Start now. This is especially important if you are working toward a specific goal. Keeping a log might hurt at first, but think of it as giving yourself credit for every moment you spend writing when you could easily be doing something else.

Part II

YOUR INNER WORLD

Your inner world is a vast region as varied and exciting as the most exotic landscape. This limitless reservoir contains all your experiences, memories, feelings, all the things you've ever seen or heard, all your ideas, fantasies, and impulses. Your inner world is a source you carry with you everywhere you go. It is always at hand, always ready to supply you with guidance, information, and creative ideas. All you have to do is ask—and then listen.

Chapter 4

———————— THE BODY ————————

Exactly where you are at this very moment, there is a house that bears your name. . . . That house, the hideaway of your most deeply buried, repressed memories, is your body.

—Thérèse Bertherat
The Body Has Its Reasons

These exercises come first in the book because they work with the primary, most tangible resource you have as a writer—your body. Your body is like a map of your existence—pockets of history, landfills of emotion—and contains clues to every experience and reaction you've had in your lifetime. The exercises will help you add viscera—bodily substance—to your writing. They can also reveal blocks and tensions and help you to work through them. The following exercises are in this section:

- *Your Laboratory*
- *A Body Symptom Speaks*
- *Recapturing a Feeling of Yourself as an Infant*
- *Scars*

Exercise 1
The Body

YOUR LABORATORY

Your body is a complex laboratory which constantly tests the environment, inside and out, and adjusts itself to the moment at hand. If you're in danger, it moves to help you; if you're tired or hungry, it sends loud signals so you'll rest or eat. The miracle that is your body performs hundreds of complex invisible activities that enable you to think, to move, to breathe, and to live. This exercise allows you to feel your body at work. The awareness of body sensations that this first exercise gives you will be important as you move through all the other exercises in the book.

Have your teacher or a friend guide you through this exercise if possible.

Close Your Eyes and Become Conscious of Your Body

Sit upright in a chair, spine straight and away from the back of the chair. Close your eyes and become aware of the physical nature of your body.

Pay Attention to Your Breathing

Notice how you are breathing. Don't try to adjust it in any way; simply notice your breathing in detail.

- ✓ Are the inhalations and exhalations both full? Is either cut short?
- ✓ Do you notice any point where you hold your breath?
- ✓ How do you visualize the shape of your breath?

Feel the Energy Flowing Through Your Body

Tune in to the current of energy that is flowing in a circuit throughout your body, from head to toe. Imagine it running from the bottom of your feet, up your arms, up the back of your spine, and to the top of your brain where it revitalizes your system.

Visualize a Specific Part of Your Body

Allow some images of different parts of your body to come to mind. For example:

- ✓ Your heart
- ✓ Your lungs
- ✓ Your throat
- ✓ Your nose

See which physical sensations you feel in specific spots.

Notice Any Shifts in Your Body Sensations

Notice if you feel any shifts in your physical sensations:

- ✓ Do you feel cooler? Warmer? More agitated? Calmer?
- ✓ Which body signals indicate these specific changes?
- ✓ Does your attention keep returning to any particular spot?

Pay Attention to Any Images That Come to Mind

- ✓ Do you see any specific images?
- ✓ If so, which parts of your body are they associated with?

28   *The Body / Your Laboratory*

Open Your Eyes but Stay Connected with Your Body

With your eyes open, feel your heart beating, your breath moving in and out, and the energy running throughout your body. Keep this state of awareness as long as possible.

✍ WRITING WARM-UP

✓ Jot down a few words to describe the experience and then discuss with one or two friends or classmates how you felt during the exercise. Compare notes and see how your experience was both like and different from their experiences.

✓ Briefly describe the main sensation or image you experienced during the exercise.

✍ WRITING ABOUT THE EXPERIENCE

✓ Take some time to think about your relationship with your body. How do you treat it? How does it respond? Write an informal analysis of the kind of relationship you have with your body.

✓ Write a history of one of your body parts—your hair, your nose, your feet, for example. Or let this body part tell the story in its own voice. Here's a good place to try some lighthearted or humorous writing.

✍ EXPANDING THE EXPERIENCE

To delve deeper into how the human body functions, consult some books on anatomy. The classic, *Gray's Anatomy*, written in 1858, is still used in medical schools today and is worth looking at; but look also at a couple of current anatomy books and see what differences you find.

✓ Choose one particular body part or organ that interests you most and conduct a thorough study of that part: how it is constructed, how it functions, what it contributes to the overall functioning of the body. Then write a paper in which you explain the process of how this body part works.

Exercise 2
The Body

A BODY SYMPTOM SPEAKS

Every symptom contains a message. Obviously if the symptom seems life-threatening, we take steps to get rid of both the symptom and the cause.

However, we probably all live with mild, chronic body disturbances which come and go at different times in our lives. Some of them disappear; others hang around indefinitely. For this exercise, choose a symptom you feel safe working with.

Relax and Become Connected with Your Breathing

Close your eyes and breathe deeply for a few moments.

Imagine Your Body Curling into a Soft Ball

After you have taken several deep breaths, exhale fully and imagine your body curling into a soft ball. Take yourself right into the middle of the soft ball.

Scan Your Body and Choose One Body Symptom

Once you are inside the ball, scan your body and remember several physical discomforts you are usually aware of. Choose one of these body symptoms to work with further.

Describe the Symptom to Yourself

Describe the symptom, avoiding all medical terms.

- ✓ What does it *feel* like?
- ✓ What do you imagine it looks like?

See if Any Visual Images Are Associated with the Symptom

If you stay with the sensations long enough, your imagination will begin to produce images. These images can give you important information about the nature of both the symptom and the cause. Stay with these images for awhile.

Think Back to When You First Experienced This Symptom

Allow your mind to travel back to when you first experienced the symptom.

- ✓ How old were you?
- ✓ What was happening in your life at this time?
- ✓ Where were you when you first noticed this symptom?

Return to the Present Images and Sensations

Continue to breathe deeply and just stay still, experiencing the images and sensations that come and go. After awhile, ask yourself these questions:

✓ What is this body symptom trying to tell me?
✓ In what ways is it useful to me?

Visualize Yourself Unfolding and Standing Up Straight

Visualize yourself uncurling from the inside of a ball and slowly unfolding outward until you see yourself standing straight up. Open your eyes slowly. See if any new sensations surround the physical problem.

✍ WRITING WARM-UP

✓ Check in with yourself to see how you are feeling. Is there any change in the body symptom at this moment? If so, write down how it feels now.

✓ List all the information you received from the body symptom during the exercise. Be sure to include any ideas for remedies that came to you.

✍ WRITING ABOUT THE EXPERIENCE

✓ Choose a person you feel comfortable with—perhaps a close friend or classmate. Explain in detail to this person everything you feel and think about the symptom. Then write a detailed journal entry in which you trace the full history of your body symptom. Include when it first appeared, how it has changed over the years, and what effect it now has on your life.

✓ Write an imaginative essay in which you allow the body symptom to speak directly to you. You can let it give you advice and information. Or perhaps you can let it justify its existence. Put yourself in its place and see what happens.

✍ EXPANDING THE EXPERIENCE

✓ If a specific physical disorder causes your body symptom, read about this disorder. Learn everything you can. Afterward, in a paper, describe the physical disorder, ending with possible solutions that you might have discovered through your research.

✓ Doctors have estimated that the largest percentage of physical symptoms are psychological or emotional in origin. If you feel that psychological or emotional responses in part cause your body symptom, look into some of the numerous books and articles available on the connection between the body and mind. One excellent book is *Quantum Healing: Exploring the Frontiers of Mind/Body Medicine* by Deepak Chopra, M.D. Write a paper reporting one major idea about how the mind affects the body.

Exercise 3	# RECAPTURING A FEELING OF
The Body	YOURSELF AS AN INFANT

Our first experiences in the world were intense nonverbal sensations, and these early sensations still reside in our bodies. In this exercise, you'll regress to recapture some of your earliest sensations and emotions from when you were an infant.

Relax Your Body

Consciously relax your mind and body by counting each inhalation and picturing your breath traveling up through your body, clearing out thoughts and tensions as you exhale. Stay with the breathing long enough to relax as much as possible.

Visualize a Baby's Tiny Body

Call up in your mind a picture of an infant and look closely at how loose and relaxed the baby's body is. Mentally try to match your body to the infant's movements for a few moments.

Picture Yourself as an Infant

You've no doubt seen photographs of yourself as an infant, but if not, imagine what you looked like.

Notice All the Physical Characteristics of Your Infant Self

Closely observe your hands and feet, your head and hair, your stomach, legs, arms, buttocks, eyes, and so forth. What age do you appear to be?

Expand Your Attention to What Is Around You

See if you can visualize anything happening around you.

✓ Where are you?
✓ Who is with you?

✓ Is anyone paying attention to you?
✓ If you're alone, can you recall any of your surroundings?

Try to Recapture Some of Your Feelings

As an infant, you perceived the world through your feelings in a direct way. You had no words. Try to capture within yourself that nonverbal state of being.

Examine One Dominant Feeling

Now zero in on one particular feeling, the one that seems most intense. Don't be too quick to give a name to it; simply allow all the different qualities that make up this feeling to coexist. Trace the feeling slowly through all the layers.

✓ What are the characteristics of it?
✓ What do you think is the source of it?
✓ In what ways does this same feeling continue in your life?

Allow the Experience to Dissolve Slowly

When you open your eyes, maintain your connection with the dominant feeling for several minutes.

✎ WRITING WARM-UP

Take a few moments to reflect on the experience. You may feel as if you were making up details and that there's no way you can remember being an infant. But current research proves that even as unborn babies, we experience the world from the womb. Whether or not you believe that, simply striving to remember yourself as an infant can add a new dimension to your personal history.

✓ With one word only, describe yourself as an infant. Then draw any kind of picture that shows how that word feels to you.

✎ WRITING ABOUT THE EXPERIENCE

✓ In as much detail as possible, write a description of yourself as an infant. Cover both the physical and emotional aspects.

✓ Write an essay or a fictional story from an infant's point of view. How do you think an infant sees the world?

✍ EXPANDING THE EXPERIENCE

The discovery that birth and early infancy are experiences that many people remember later in life is fairly new. Two major books that appeared in the 1970s still stand as the most important in the field:

> Birth Without Violence by Frederic Leboyer looks at birth from an infant's point of view. The Leboyer method has dramatically transformed birth delivery.
> The Secret Life of the Unborn Child by Dr. Thomas Verny presents scientific information that proves that the unborn child is responsive to the surrounding environment.

If this subject interests you, you might want to read these books and others in the field. These two writing suggestions can help you explore the subject in depth:

✓ Discuss how birth practices have changed in the past 50 years. How does your delivery into the world compare with your siblings', your parents', and your grandparents'?

✓ Explain each important stage in a child's life from birth to two years of age. What obstacles must a child overcome in order to survive into early childhood?

Exercise 4
The Body
SCARS

The minute you saw this title, a response probably jumped into your head. All of us are keenly aware of our scars. You might have thought of emotional scars or actual physical ones. The exercise works with a physical scar, but you can also adapt it to emotional or psychological scars.

Close Your Eyes and Make a Mental Run-through of All the Scars on Your Body

Take your time and scan your entire body slowly. You'll probably remember a few scars you haven't thought about in awhile.

Briefly Remember the History of Each of Your Scars

Think about each of them:

✓ How did you acquire it?
✓ At what age?
✓ What's most significant about it?

34 *The Body / Scars*

Choose One Particular Scar to Work With

- ✓ What special qualities does this scar have above the others?
- ✓ Is this a scar you've paid attention to before now?

Remember Back to When, Where, and How You Acquired It

Think more about getting the scar.

- ✓ Where were you?
- ✓ How old were you?
- ✓ What caused the scar?

Put Yourself into the Moment and Relive It

Go back through the events leading to the moment when you got the scar:

- ✓ What happened immediately beforehand?
- ✓ Who else is involved? What part do they play?
- ✓ What part do you play?
- ✓ What are you doing at the moment the scar happens?
- ✓ How do you feel?

Open Your Eyes and Imagine the Scar as It Looks Right Now

Without looking at it, see if you can remember exactly what it looks like.

- ✓ How would you describe it?
- ✓ Has it changed in any way since you first got it?
- ✓ Has it caused you any problems?
- ✓ How do you feel about it now?

———— ■ ————

✍ WRITING WARM-UP

Take some time to come back into the present. Check in and see how you feel now.

- ✓ Have your feelings toward the scar changed in any way? Write a short journal entry exploring your feelings about the scar.
- ✓ Draw an outline of your body and indicate with an X each place where you have a scar. Draw some of the scars in more detail if you like.

The Body 35

✍ WRITING ABOUT THE EXPERIENCE

Scars are fascinating subjects. For some reason, people seem to enjoy hearing stories about causes of scars. With a group of friends or classmates, exchange scar stories. Telling your story aloud and hearing others' stories will give you ideas for writing.

✓ After the exchange of stories, write a narrative account of how you acquired the scar. Don't tell too much about what happened before and after. Concentrate on the actual event and turn it into a dramatic retelling.

✓ Write a personal essay about all the major scars you have acquired. Tell what they are (they can be physical, psychological, or emotional) and how your feel about each of them. If one scar seems more important than the others, give that scar emphasis in your paper.

✍ EXPANDING THE EXPERIENCE

The *American Heritage Dictionary of the English Language* defines a "scar" as: "A lingering sign of damage or injury, either mental or physical." But scars are also considered marks of accomplishment—such as proof of survival, evidence of triumph, or badges of bravery.

✓ Think about your own scar in these terms. What evidence is behind it? What does it prove about you in terms of survival, endurance, or bravery? With a small group of friends or classmates, discuss this aspect of scars and see what emerges after looking at scars from this angle. Then write a paper that champions your scar as proof of some strength of character.

✓ Stephen Crane's short novel, *The Red Badge of Courage,* is probably the most well-known work that endows a wound (or scar) with symbolic meaning. If you'd like to explore the idea further, read Crane's novel and some critical writings about the work. The Norton Critical Edition contains both the novel and critical essays. Then write a paper focusing on the wound itself: how Henry Fleming acquires the wound—his "red badge of courage"—and what it means to him symbolically. Or, using scars as your organizing idea, you can write a paper about a number of other characters from literature or film who have prominent scars.

Chapter 5

—— CHILDHOOD —— MEMORIES

I was gathering images all of my life, storing them away, and forgetting them. Somehow I had to send myself back, with words as catalysts, to open the memories out and see what they had to offer.

—Ray Bradbury
Preface, Dandelion Wine

Most of the exercises in this book are based on some kind of remembering. But this section—and the one that follows—is about *memory*, that vast storehouse which provides most of a writer's material. Looking back, childhood seems to have stretched on forever. Time was long. We had idle hours in which to savor the days. We had new eyes with which to see the world for the first time. No wonder childhood memories rush in on us so often and so vividly. These exercises will help you pull out some childhood memories, a piece at a time, and polish them up with adult meaning.

- *First Love*
- *Grown-ups*
- *Family Snapshot*
- *I Remember*

Exercise 1
Childhood
Memories

FIRST LOVE

Sometimes a first love can set the stage for all future loves. Going back to that earliest love and your feelings then might give you some insights into all your other loves throughout the years—and now.

Childhood Memories 37

Think Back to the Very First Time You Felt Heart Palpitations for Someone Else

Perhaps your first love was someone in your own family. If so, work with that person if you can't recall your earliest boyfriend or girlfriend. But go back as far in time as possible to an early heartthrob.

Close Your Eyes and Put the Face of Your First Love Before Your Inner Eye

Let the image of your first love grow large, as if on a giant TV screen. Stay with it until you get a clear picture of the person.

Look Closely at the Physical Details of This Person

Look straight into the eyes of your first love.

- ✓ Look at all the physical details of the other person—hair, teeth, nose, clothes, and so forth.
- ✓ What attracted you most about this person?
- ✓ See him or her moving around. Notice any unusual gestures.

Recollect a Specific Time You Were Together

Now recollect a time you were together and trace the incident as fully as you can.

- ✓ How old were you? How old was your first love?
- ✓ Where were you? What were you doing?
- ✓ How did you feel in the company of your first love?

Identify Any Other Events Connected with This Early Love

Think about other times, places, and people you associate with your first love.

- ✓ How often were you together?
- ✓ Were other people involved in any way?
- ✓ Do any important events stand out?

Trace the History of This First Love Affair

Follow this love affair from beginning to end. Even if it was just puppy love, your feelings were as important to you then as they are today.

✓ How did the relationship progress? Over how many years?
✓ How did the relationship finally end?
✓ When was the last time you saw your first love?

Let Your Memories Dissolve and Return to the Present

Take a moment more to think about this person.

✓ Where is he or she now?
✓ In retrospect, what was your most persistent feeling throughout the relationship?

✍ WRITING WARM-UP

✓ If your first love were here right now in front of your eyes, what would you say to him or her? Write down what you would say.

✓ In a few sentences, describe the dominant feeling you had during the relationship. In what ways does that feeling still linger in your life?

✍ WRITING ABOUT THE EXPERIENCE

✓ Write a paper in which you subordinate the relationship itself to a more major idea: what you learned about romantic relationships from your first love. How was it similar to other romantic relationships you've had since becoming an adult?

✓ Write a paper about love from the point of view of a young person. You can take it from a child's point of view, or from a young adolescent's. If children "in love" could explain their feelings, what do you think they would say? A famous song on the subject is "Too Young," made popular by Nat King Cole many years ago. It should be easy to find a recording of the song and listen to the lyrics to spark some ideas for your paper.

✍ EXPANDING THE EXPERIENCE

✓ Take some time to compare first love stories with two or three classmates or friends. After you've each described your first love, focus the discussion on common patterns you shared. How are these early romantic experiences alike? After the discussion, write a paper which analyzes some of the meanings of first love, using your own experience as the main example. Don't, however, make this paper merely another narrative account of your own personal experience: Put it in a larger context and discuss the universal qualities of your experience.

✓ Another enjoyable project would be to survey first love experiences in literature. Concentrate on a particular genre—such as poems, short stories, novels, or plays—and collect a number for one group only. In that case, you would read several poems, short stories, or the like, and then report how different authors have handled this theme. Another way to conduct the survey would be to focus on one idea about the first love experience and then set out to prove your idea by tracing it through different types of literature. A good place to begin your search is to use "First Love" as your subject and find titles by that name. (For example, Ivan Turgenev has written a short novel entitled *First Love* and Harold Brodkey has a short story entitled "First Love and Other Sorrows." There are many others.) After the initial search, you can go further and seek other works based on this theme, but with different titles. Ask your teacher and other classmates for recommendations.

Exercise 2
Childhood
Memories

Grown-ups

Many childhood events seem to have occurred totally in a child's world, a world without grown-ups. And yet the grown-ups were always there behind the scenes, directing the show—and many times walking right onto the stage and interrupting the action. You no doubt remember some of those times when you were doing just fine until the grown-ups showed up.

Think About Some of the Grown-ups You Knew as a Child

Take a few minutes to make a mental list of all the grown-ups who peopled your life when you were a child.

✓ What was their relationship to you?
✓ How did you feel about them?

Close Your Eyes and Travel Backward in Time

When you have a few grown-ups in mind, close your eyes, take several deep breaths, and imagine yourself going backward in time. Visualize yourself becoming progressively younger until you see yourself as a child under the age of six or seven.

Visualize Yourself Playing and Having Fun

See yourself doing all the things you enjoyed as a child.

- ✓ What were some of your favorite games?
- ✓ Who were the other children you played with?
- ✓ How did you feel when you were playing and having fun?

Remember the Grown-ups in Your Life at This Point

Visualize most of the important grown-ups in your life at this time.

- ✓ What part did they play in your life?
- ✓ How did you feel about them individually?
- ✓ How did you feel about grown-ups in general?

Recall an Incident with a Grown-up

This incident can be one in which the grown-up interfered and upset you or it can be one in which you enjoyed the company of a grown-up. See the incident from start to finish.

- ✓ Where are you?
- ✓ Who is the grown-up with you?
- ✓ What happens?
- ✓ How do you feel at the moment?

Connect This Incident with Your General Feelings About Grown-ups

- ✓ How did this incident shape your attitudes about grown-ups at the time?
- ✓ How did your attitude change over the years?
- ✓ What is your attitude now toward grown-ups?

Before Opening Your Eyes, See Yourself Both as a Child and as a Grown-up

See yourself growing up over the years until you become your present age. When you open your eyes, continue to maintain awareness of yourself both as a child and a grown-up.

———■———

✍ WRITING WARM-UP

✓ In a sentence or two, describe the kind of child you were and the kind of grown-up you've become.

✓ Draw a line down the middle of the page. On the left, list words that describe grown-ups; on the right, list words that describe children. Compare the two lists.

✍ WRITING ABOUT THE EXPERIENCE

✓ Write an essay explaining the opinion you held of grown-ups when you were a child. Support your opinion with examples from your own childhood experiences with grown-ups. Then bring the essay into the present by describing the kind of adult you've become and show the connection between your childhood opinions and the ones you hold now. Have you turned out as you thought you would when you were a child?

✓ Try your hand at writing a humorous essay about what it means to be a grown-up, something like "How to Act Like a Grown-up."

✍ EXPANDING THE EXPERIENCE

Antoine de Saint-Exupéry, in the dedication to *The Little Prince,* his classic tale much loved by both children and adults, says "All grown-ups were once children—although few of them remember it." And, in fact, the book is an indictment against the grown-up vision that lacks creativity and spontaneity. In the opening chapter, the narrator describes a time when he was six years old and drew pictures of a boa constrictor swallowing an animal. He keeps showing his drawings to the adults but none of them can see what he is trying to draw. They discourage him. Finally he gives up trying to draw and learns to pilot airplanes. He says, "I have lived a great deal among grown-ups. I have seen them intimately, close at hand. And that hasn't much improved my opinion of them."

✓ To recapture some of your childhood spirit and imagination, read *The Little Prince* or a favorite book from your childhood. Discuss with a small group of classmates or friends the books you loved and how these books affected your imagination. Perhaps even bring the books to exchange and look at, if you still have them. Afterward, write an essay exploring the ways it is possible to maintain or regain childhood creativity and imagination as an adult. To give substance to your paper, read books about theories of creativity, such as Rollo May's *The Courage to Create.*

Exercise 3
Childhood
Memories

FAMILY SNAPSHOT

You can do this exercise many times, using a snapshot from every period of your life to rediscover important feelings you had about yourself and others at that time. Seeing yourself in old snapshots can bring up a lot of buried—sometimes very emotional—memories, so go gently with yourself on this one.

Put Yourself into a Relaxed Mood

In preparation for the exercise, take a few moments to close your eyes and relax yourself by taking several deep breaths and imagining them circling through your brain, wiping out all thoughts. Concentrate on relaxing your eyes completely.

Pick Out an Old Photograph of Yourself from Any Period in Your Life

An informal snapshot is ideal, but if all you have is a formal studio portrait, that's fine. If you can actually hold the photo in your hands, do so. If not, just visualize one you remember. And if memory fails, or you have no photographs, use your imagination to create one, perhaps one you wish had been taken.

Study the Photograph Closely

If you have the photograph in hand, you can use a magnifying glass to study the small details. If you don't have an actual photograph, use the one you remember or imagine and mentally project it enlarged onto a screen so that you can look at all the details.

Observe the Setting

- ✓ Is it indoors or outdoors?
- ✓ What season of the year is it?
- ✓ What time of day?
- ✓ What are the specific surroundings within the frame of the photo?
- ✓ What is outside the frame?

Look at Who Else and What Else Is in the Photograph

- ✓ If you're not alone in the photo, who are the other people? Take a long slow look at all the others.

✓ Is anybody missing from this snapshot?
✓ Who do you think took the picture?

Look at What Else Is in the Photograph

✓ Are there any animals in the photo?
✓ Are there any important inanimate objects in it?
✓ Is anything missing from the picture?

Examine Yourself in Detail

✓ What are you doing in the picture?
✓ Look at the expression on your face; notice what you're wearing.
✓ See if you can remember exactly what was going on in your life at this time.
✓ Look into your eyes and see if you can remember what you were feeling at the time of the photo.
✓ Can you remember wanting something from someone—something you either got or did not?

Recall What Happened Right Before and Right After the Snapshot

✓ Did anything significant occur during or after the snapshot?
✓ Where were other members of the family when this shot was taken?
✓ Were they conscious of you—of what you were doing and feeling?

Put the Photograph Aside or Allow Its Image to Dissolve

If you used an actual photograph for the exercise, put it aside. If you imagined one, open your eyes at this point. Spend a few moments reseeing the photograph and feeling the impact of the exercise.

✓ How did you feel during the exercise?
✓ Did you see anything you had not remembered seeing before?

———————■———————

✍ WRITING WARM-UP

✓ Draw a layout of the photograph, indicating with symbols the placement of each person, animal, or important object.

✓ In a few sentences explain what is outside the frame of the photograph and why it is significant—in other words, why do you still remember it even though it's not in the snapshot?

✍ WRITING ABOUT THE EXPERIENCE

✓ Narrate the story of the taking of the photograph. Don't stop to wonder whether you're making up some of the story. Chances are your perceptions are true no matter how fictional they may seem.

✓ Describe yourself on the day of the photograph. Who were you then? What was unusual about you? Tell what you remember about how you felt, what you wanted, and what you got or didn't get.

✍ EXPANDING THE EXPERIENCE

Photographs of people you know, as well as people you don't know, are excellent story-starters. Simply examining a photograph—or painting—will raise questions and ideas in your head. And these questions and ideas can lead you to inventing your own story.

✓ Write a story from an objective point of view about the people in your photograph. See them as "characters." What does each of them want? What's in the way of getting what they want? Use your family snapshot to begin the story. The following passage, part of the opening paragraph from *The Pursuit of Love,* a novel by Nancy Mitford, might help you begin your own story:

There is a photograph in existence of Aunt Sadie and her six children sitting round the tea-table at Alconleigh. The table is situated as it was, is now, and ever shall be, in the hall, in front of a huge open fire of logs. . . . In the photograph Aunt Sadie's face, always beautiful, appears strangely round, her hair strangely fluffy, and her clothes strangely dowdy, but it is unmistakably she who sits there with Robin, in oceans of lace, lolling on her knee. She seems uncertain what to do with his head, and the presence of Nanny waiting to take him away is felt though not seen. The other children, between Louisa's eleven and Matt's two years, sit round the table in party dresses or frilly bibs, holding cups or mugs according to age, all of them gazing at the camera with large eyes opened wide by the flash, and all looking as if butter would not melt in their round pursed-up mouths. There they are, held like flies in the amber of that moment—click goes the camera and on goes life. . . .

✓ Study a famous painting or photograph which portrays a group of people or a single person. Write the story of this painting or photograph as you imagine it. Afterward, do some reading and learn all you can about the historical events and people. How did the photograph or painting come into existence? What is significant about it? Write a paper telling the actual story behind this painting or photograph. Contrast your prior ideas with the ones you developed after you gained new information.

Exercise 4
Childhood
Memories

I REMEMBER

Everything that has ever happened to you is still stored in your memory waiting for you to reclaim it. The purpose of this exercise is to take you as far back as you can remember, to your very earliest memory—perhaps even to the moment when you first became aware of being alive.

Set your sights on going back to the preverbal stage of your development, but don't criticize yourself if you can make it back only to grade school or even high school years. As you get your memory flowing, you'll go further back each time you do the exercise.

The first time you do this exercise, have someone read it to you so that you can concentrate on going back as far as you can. After you are familiar with the exercise, you can do it on your own.

Get into a Comfortable Position and Close Your Eyes

Take a few moments to become totally relaxed in order to put yourself into a receptive frame of mind. Do the spiral breathing several times before beginning.

Visualize Yourself on an Elevator, Descending to an Earlier Age

Imagine yourself entering an elevator. You are on the 18th floor. The buttons on the elevator number from 18 to B, representing the first 18 years of your life.

✓ Push a button between 18 and 12 and feel yourself descend to that "floor"—that age in your life.
✓ When the elevator doors open, step out to the floor and remember yourself at that age.

Retrieve a Memory of Yourself at That Age

Take whatever memory comes to you about that particular age. It can be something as simple as a dress or suit you wore or a remembered snapshot.

Get Back on the Elevator and Push a Lower Button

Get back on the elevator and push another button between 12 and 6. Visualize yourself going down gently and safely. When the doors open, step out into that age and retrieve another memory. Bring it back with you and get on the elevator again.

When You're Back on the Elevator, Push a Button Lower than Six

If possible, go down in the elevator as far as one or two—or even to "B" for basement. Feel yourself descend slowly, floor by floor, into the safe darkness. When the elevator stops, get out and walk around and see what comes to you.

Choose One of These Early Memories to Work With

When you have retrieved a memory that seems important to you, stay with it and keep visualizing it.

- ✓ Where are you?
- ✓ Who's with you?
- ✓ How are you feeling?
- ✓ What kinds of colors and shapes do you see around you?
- ✓ What sounds and smells?
- ✓ What are you most aware of?

Stay with the Scene Until You Have Retrieved Buried Details

If you continue to watch the scene with your eyes closed, many other details will come into view.

- ✓ What is going on around you? What do you notice that you did not notice before?
- ✓ What can you hear others saying?
- ✓ At what point does the scene end?

Return to the Elevator and Come Back Slowly to the Surface, Bringing with You the Memories You Retrieved

Get back on the elevator, allow the doors to close, and push the button marked 18. Feel the elevator rise floor by floor. Take your time returning. Before opening your eyes, ask yourself these questions:

✓ Why is this particular memory important to me?

✓ What does it still evoke in me?

✍ WRITING WARM-UP

✓ Write one sentence that gives your age and the exact event that took place: "When I was _____ years old, ..."

✓ Write a few sentences describing how the process of the exercise affected you. Did you recall an event you thought you had forgotten? Did any of the details surprise you?

✍ WRITING ABOUT THE EXPERIENCE

✓ Narrate the event that you remembered most vividly during the exercise. Write about one short incident—something that happened within minutes. Use the present tense as if it's happening in the moment. Tell it from a child's point of view and capture in writing the things you saw, heard, and felt: "I'm in my high chair. I can see my dog Fluffy running around outside in the yard. I want to go outside and play with her. . . . " The big challenge in writing this narrative will be to maintain a child's view. If you get off track, close your eyes and go back to the memory for a few seconds.

✓ Write a family story about yourself that others have told you but which you do not remember experiencing. You have no doubt heard it several times, perhaps from more than one person. First tell your favorite version of it; then include the other versions and show how they differ. End your story by analyzing why you like this story about yourself. What does it show about you as a person?

✍ EXPANDING THE EXPERIENCE

✓ With a small group of friends, trade early memories. Discuss among yourselves the process of regression and evaluate your success in retrieving early memories. Talk about selective memory—why you remember some minor events while you forget larger ones. Why did you remember this particular event, for example? Why is it still important to you? Afterward, write an essay that describes the event and then explains its importance in your development as an adult. Don't be too quick to dismiss the event as meaningless. Keep probing until you find a connection between then and now.

✓ Carl Jung and Sigmund Freud, two of the most prominent founders of modern psychotherapy, both proved through their work that early childhood experiences—even seemingly insignificant ones—have profound effects on our lives as adults. Jung said that our earliest memory is often a key to understanding ourselves as adults. Read selectively on the subject of early childhood memories. This field is vast, however, so limit yourself to one or two theories. You might be interested in more recent theories, such as those of Karen Horney, Alice Miller, R. D. Laing, or John Bradshaw. After you've studied the subject, write an essay in which you present and explain one major idea about early childhood memories. Use your own experience as an example if possible.

Chapter 6

——— MEMORABLE ———
MOMENTS

There seems something else in life besides time, something which may conveniently be called "value," something which is measured not by minutes or hours, but by intensity, so that when we look at our past it does not stretch back evenly but piles up into a few notable pinnacles.

—E. M. Forster
Aspects of the Novel

The moments that stand out in our memory are not always the grand and important ones. Sometimes we remember a tiny moment that has particular significance for us alone. The moment can be a happy one or a sad one; we might have been with others or by ourselves. But somehow the moment takes its place among our store of memories and presents itself to us to remember, to relive, perhaps to reexamine. The following four exercises will help you look more closely at a few of your own such moments:

- *A Memorable Prank*
- *A Moment of Rebellion*
- *An Eating Experience*
- *Water*

Exercise 1
Memorable
Moments

A MEMORABLE PRANK

Pulling off a prank, either alone or with a group of others, is generally remembered with pleasure and as a special moment. You've no doubt been part of some pranks others would enjoy laughing about. The prank might be as simple as taking someone on a snipe hunt or as elaborate as stealing an alligator from the zoo and putting it into a friend's bathtub. Your intention in describing the prank, however big or small, is to entertain your audience with humorous storytelling.

Have Fun by Musing on All the Pranks You Can Remember

You might have been the instigator, a participant, or even an innocent by-stander. Enjoy the memory of any pranks that you can remember, and feel the pleasure and laughter inside yourself. Make a quick list, if you like.

Choose One of the Pranks to Study in Detail

It can be one you observed or one you participated in.

Close Your Eyes and Visualize It Taking Place Start to Finish

✓ Where and when does it take place?
✓ Who are the people, animals, or objects involved?
✓ How does the prank begin?
✓ How does it end?

Zero In on the Chief Actor

✓ Who instigated the prank?
✓ Why? What was the motivation for it?

Pinpoint the Funniest Moment

✓ Where does the climax of the prank come?
✓ Is any new element introduced at this point? If so, what?
✓ How does this moment affect the people involved?
✓ How does this moment affect the bystanders?

Think About Why This Moment Was the Funniest

Look backward to the setup: What earlier elements combined to make this moment the funniest?

✓ Did some twist in events or action occur?
✓ Was an unexpected element introduced?
✓ What ultimately enabled the prankster to succeed?

Open Your Eyes and Think Briefly About the Effects of the Prank

✓ Was this a harmful prank or harmless?
✓ Were there any consequences?

✐ WRITING WARM-UP

✓ List all the pranks you've either witnessed or been part of. Add a few you've heard about and some you'd like to do.

✓ List all the ingredients you think are necessary for a successful prank.

✐ WRITING ABOUT THE EXPERIENCE

✓ Put the story into writing. Make it as funny as possible. (Would what you've written make someone else laugh?) You can narrate the story like this: Begin with the funniest moment and then explain how it all came about. Or, if you prefer to tell the prank chronologically, be certain to give the climax the most development in your writing. Be sure that the "punch" comes through.

✓ Write a paper expressing your opinion about whether the prank was harmless or harmful. Defend your position with as much evidence as possible. Use the events of the prank to illustrate your points.

✐ EXPANDING THE EXPERIENCE

✓ With a group of classmates or friends, conduct an inquiry into the nature of pranks. Swap prank stories and then look at the motivation behind some of them. Are any of the pranks cruel? Are any of the pranks harmful? Why do pranks appeal so universally to people? What human need do they answer? You shouldn't come up with a group consensus. Instead, form your own conclusions about pranks. After you've got a clear view of your own opinion, write a paper either defending or criticizing pranks.

Exercise 2
Memorable
Moments

A MOMENT OF REBELLION

A thin line exists between sticking up for yourself and being all-out rebellious. Most of us as children felt some rebellion against the authority of others—parents, other relatives, or teachers—and sometimes did forbidden things to satisfy this rebellion. But the need for rebellion doesn't end with childhood. It stays with us for life and, whether or not we actually rebel, we often feel the need to do so—to say no to demands, to walk out on a job, to fight encroachments on our freedom, or to turn things upside down for the pleasure of it.

Assess the Way You Were as a Child

✓ Were you rebellious by nature?
✓ Were you basically obedient? If so, did you have a few moments in which you felt rebellious?

Reflect on Any Incidents from Your Childhood in Which You Defied Authority

Close your eyes and travel slowly backward through the years. Think about some of the times you did things you weren't supposed to do. If you can't think of anything you actually did, think about things you *wanted* to rebel against.

Now Reflect on Some Rebellious Incidents in Your Life as an Adult

Take your time and go through your life a few years at a time until you have a few incidents.

Choose One Specific Incident to Work With

Pick an incident to work with from either your childhood or since you've been an adult. The incident can be one in which you either refused to do something you were told to do or you did something you knew you were not supposed to do.

Relive the Event

Locate the event in time and space.

✓ Where are you?
✓ Who is with you?
✓ What's going on?
✓ How old are you?

Focus on the Moment When You Decided to Disobey

Go to the center of the event and look in detail at the moment when you decided to disobey authority.

✓ Who are you rebelling against? Why?
✓ Did anyone else influence you?
✓ What motivated you to rebel?

Reflect on the Consequences of Your Act

- ✓ Did you get away with your prank?
- ✓ Were you found out?
- ✓ Did you receive any punishment?
- ✓ What was the final result?

Replay the Event

This time when you go over each part of the event, stay aware of your body and how it feels.

- ✓ How did you feel when you were being disobedient?
- ✓ Where in your body do you still feel that defiance?
- ✓ How do you feel about the event in retrospect?

———————■———————

✎ WRITING WARM-UP

- ✓ In a few sentences, summarize your current feelings about the forbidden act you recalled. Would you do it again?

- ✓ List all the things you'd like right now to rebel against.

✎ WRITING ABOUT THE EXPERIENCE

- ✓ Write a narrative account of your rebellion. Keep in mind your current feelings about it. End with an explanation of how this incident is evidence of your deeper feelings and attitudes.

- ✓ Who has authority over you now? Write about a specific person you feel currently has authority over you and why he or she has this authority. Explain how you feel about the situation and what (if anything) you plan to do about it.

✎ EXPANDING THE EXPERIENCE

There's clear evidence of how destructive the committing of forbidden acts can be to a society. The news is full of such acts—robberies, assaults, drug deals, political intrigue, and financial scams. Sometimes, however, disobeying laws and rules can be an effective statement. Sometimes doing so can even save your life.

- ✓ Think of times when taking action forbidden by law, church, or some other authority figure in your life could benefit you. For example, the followers of Jim Jones (the leader of a group in British Guyana who ordered mass suicide in 1978) would have saved their lives had they acted contrary to his orders. Read about events such as this. Choose one example and write an essay in which you prove that in that particular case, rebelling against authority would have been justified.

✓ The course of history would be far different had people not engaged in rebellious acts for what they considered a greater cause. Many famous leaders have advocated refusal to comply with laws as a way to bring about social change. Seek out some of the most famous documents that support this position, such as Thomas Paine's *Common Sense,* Henry David Thoreau's *Civil Disobedience,* and Martin Luther King's "Letter from Birmingham City Jail." After some personal reflection, write an essay in which you take a position either for or against the use of civil disobedience to attain higher goals. Use examples from history to prove your point.

Exercise 3
Memorable
Moments
AN EATING EXPERIENCE

Food—that most basic ingredient for life. Sometimes it's scarce, sometimes plentiful. Sometimes we love it; sometimes we hate it. Sometimes it's our friend; sometimes our enemy. But like it or not, we all have to eat it. And many of our moments with food are indelibly inscribed in our memories.

Take a Few Minutes to Relax and Then Focus on Your Stomach

Take a few deep breaths, relax, and tune into the sensations in your stomach—how it feels when it's empty; how it feels when it's full; and how it feels right now.

Close Your Eyes and Visualize the Last Thing You Ate

What did you last eat and when? Visualize it fully. See yourself eating it, paying attention to the texture, the smell, and the taste.

✓ How did it feel in your mouth?
✓ How did it feel going down your throat?
✓ How did it feel in your stomach shortly after you ate it and then much later?
✓ How was this alike or different from the way you usually feel after eating something?

Do a Quick Review of Your Relationship to Food

Think back over your life and the different feelings and attitudes you've had toward food. Take time to pinpoint any changes you've made in these attitudes over the years.

- ✓ How did you feel about food when you were a child?
- ✓ Were there particular foods you hated or loved?
- ✓ What kind of relationship do you have to food as an adult?
- ✓ Are there foods you especially dislike or like?

Now Take Yourself Back to a Truly Memorable Experience You Once Had with Food

After you have a sense of your relationship with food, think of a memorable eating experience. The experience can be one you enjoyed or disliked.

- ✓ Locate the experience in time and place. If you're with others, put them into the picture.
- ✓ Place the food in front of you and recapture the experience. See the colors, the textures, and how it is served.
- ✓ Imagine yourself tasting it once again. Think of words to describe exactly how it tastes.

Observe Yourself Eating

- ✓ How do you feel as you eat?
- ✓ How do you actually eat the food? See yourself clearly.
- ✓ What major tastes stand out?

Let the Scene Dissolve and Open Your Eyes

After you open your eyes, remain conscious of your stomach and the eating experience you just recreated. Reflect for a moment on why this experience with food was memorable.

—————■—————

✍ WRITING WARM-UP

- ✓ Sum up your relationship with food in a few sentences that explain your primary relationship with it.

- ✓ In a paragraph, explain how the experience you recreated in the exercise characterizes your usual experience with food, and how it differs.

✍ WRITING ABOUT THE EXPERIENCE

✓ Write a detailed description of the experience. Set the stage: where you were, whom you were with, and what you ate. Focus in detail on the colors, textures, and tastes of the food—make the food important to the telling. Conclude with why this eating experience was so memorable.

✓ Choose a food that you love intensely and write a brief history of your love affair with it. Go back to your discovery of this food, your early days with it, and then bring up to the present your feelings about this food. How have they changed over the years?

✍ EXPANDING THE EXPERIENCE

Food, eating, and cooking all occupy a big chunk of our daily lives—if we're among the fortunate ones. But the large majority of people in the world go to bed hungry or eventually die from malnutrition. Although many organizations have struggled for years to end world hunger, the flow of food hasn't changed much—most of it remains in the hands of a small percentage of the global population. Only a few of us consistently have enough healthful food to eat.

If this topic interests you, undertake a study of world hunger. Use books, articles, documentaries, and movies to gather specific information about the current situation. A source of annual statistics about world population and the global environment is *State of the World: A Worldwatch Institute Report on Progress Toward a Sustainable Society,* which you can get in the reference section of a library.

✓ After some research and reading, write an essay in which you present the facts and then devote the rest of your essay to suggestions for how we might remedy the hunger situations—either in this country or in the world. In your suggestions for solutions, include any current projects that you think are helping.

✓ Write a personal-experience paper based on an experiment: Go without food for one day; volunteer to serve for a day in a soup kitchen; or work for a day with a local organization whose chief concern is ending hunger. In your paper, tell about your experience and what you learned about yourself and others.

✓ America, which has one of the world's most abundant food supplies, also has a high rate of eating disorders such as anorexia and bulimia. Through research (which might include interviews with professionals in the field), discover the connection between these two facts. When did eating disorders become such a health issue? Why are they more prevalent in this country?

WATER

Water, one of the four elements necessary for our survival, covers 70 percent of the earth's surface. All of us began our lives surrounded by water in the womb and our bodies are composed primarily of water. We could not live many days without it. Who has not experienced the soothing effects of a hot bath or the blessings of cool water on a parched throat? But not all water experiences are pleasant ones. Some of us have battled for our lives in the depths of rivers and oceans. This exercise gets you thinking about water in general and then zeroes in on a particular experience.

Close Your Eyes and Allow Different Images of Water to Come into Your Mind

Reflect on the many different forms of water that you know: a waterfall, a glass of water, a river, rain, water in a bathtub, ice cubes, melting snow, and so on. Take time to visualize different forms of water and their particular characteristics.

Think About All the Ways We Depend on Water

Consider how we use water and depend upon it.

- ✓ What are different ways we use it?
- ✓ What happens when there is too much or not enough?
- ✓ What symbols and rituals do we associate with it?

Recall Some of the Characteristics You Associate with Water

What adjectives and comparisons come to mind when you think about water in all its different forms?

Think About Your Own Relationship to Water

Think about water in terms of yourself.

- ✓ What is your favorite form of water?
- ✓ How does it affect you?
- ✓ Does any form of water frighten you?
- ✓ How would you characterize your relationship with water?

Relive a Few Experiences You've Had with Water

Briefly run through some of your experiences with water. (They can be either pleasant or frightening moments.)

Choose One of These Experiences to Remember in Detail

Pick one of your experiences with water to work with.

- ✓ What kind of water is it?
- ✓ Where are you?
- ✓ When is it?
- ✓ Who is with you?

Relive the Experience Completely

Take several deep breaths and think about your experience in detail.

- ✓ From start to finish, what happened? Slowly relive every moment you can remember.

———————■———————

✍ WRITING WARM-UP

- ✓ List all the forms of water that you can think of. Make each item as specific as possible. Put a star by those that are special to you. (To spur your memory, think back to images you remember from film or literature.)

- ✓ As you reflect upon the experience you had in the exercise, think about your relationship to water in general. Have you had many important moments with water? Does it hold special meaning for you? After this reflection, write a paragraph that describes your relationship with water.

✍ WRITING ABOUT THE EXPERIENCE

- ✓ Write a short paper narrating the experience you had with water. Why does this experience stand out in your mind? Recapture the qualities of this particular water and the nature of your relationship to it. Did this event change your relationship with water in any way? If so, conclude your paper with an explanation of the meaning of this change.

✓ Try your hand at writing a short poem entitled "Water." Keep it under 12 lines and use free verse—no rhyme or meter. The idea is to try to capture your water experience in a few vivid sentences.

✍ EXPANDING THE EXPERIENCE

To immerse yourself in an imaginary water experience that will delight all your senses, listen to a recording of Claude Debussy's *La Mer* (*The Sea*). (A good recording is *Debussy La Mer/Three Nocturnes* with Carlo Maria Giulini conducting the Philharmonic Orchestra.) Do this alone or share the music with a group of friends so you can later compare the experience.

✓ Play the piece through (it takes 25 minutes) and simply listen. Become aware of all the spontaneous images that arise in your mind as you listen to each of the three movements. Tune into the changing moods as the music progresses. The titles of the movements themselves create poetic images: "From Dawn to Noon at Sea," "Play of the Waves," and "Dialogue Between the Wind and the Sea."

Now replay the piece and begin to write, letting the music shape your writing. Really let yourself go and be guided by the music sweeping through you. Play the piece several times as you keep writing. After you've taken your journey, review your writing for common images and themes. Do you see any unifying threads? Is there a way you could add unification to what you've written and turn it into a full-length essay? Read what you've written to others for their response. Later, you can turn the writing into a piece of imaginative writing.

✓ *Water* is only one of the four elements essential to sustaining life. The other three are *earth, fire,* and *air.* Think about the significance of the other three elements and, using the ideas in this exercise, recreate a memorable experience you had with either earth, fire, or air. Write an essay about that experience, illustrating the vital necessity of that particular element. If you have the time and interest, find scientific writings about the element and include some of that information in your essay.

✓ Native Americans have absolute reverence and appreciation for all the elements that support life. A Native American custom that makes actual and symbolic use of the four elements is the *sweat lodge* (sometimes called the stone people's lodge), an ancient, highly ritualized healing ceremony. Read about the origins and current practices of the sweat lodge—what it signifies, and how it is carried out. Use this information as the basis for a paper in which you explain, using both words and visuals, how and why this ceremony is conducted.

✓ Because they are forces necessary to our existence, the four elements are full of symbolic significance for us. Art and literature consistently use the four elements as themes, images, and symbols. Organize a group discussion and brainstorm about the literature—films, poems, plays, short stories, and novels—or works of art that use one of the four elements in a significant way. Then choose one literary or art form and study it closely looking specifically for references and images centered around one of the elements. If you want to turn this into a group project, plan an oral presentation centered around one writer or artist. Each member of the group can present one work, using readings from literary works (for a writer) or illustrations (for an artist), therein giving a broad view of the writer or artist's work. If you prefer to do an individual project, choose one piece by the writer or artist and do a close study of the use of the element. Then write a paper explaining your observations. You may read outside sources for ideas later, but first conduct your own study and see what you discover.

Chapter 7

——— INTENSE ———
EMOTIONS

Denying one's feelings doesn't make them go away. Nor can one overcome a feeling which is really an aspect of the self.

—Alexander Lowen
Fear of Life

"Negative" emotions—feelings most people would prefer not to have—are easier to use than get rid of. Strong feelings have supplied many writers and other artists with valuable material, and they can do the same for you. These exercises take you back to moments of intense, sometimes painful, emotion so that you can go past any blocks you have and then reshape the experiences in a productive way. This section includes the following exercises:

- *Early Rejection*
- *A Throw-It-in-the-Fire Confession*
- *The Angry Exercise*
- *Jealousy*

Exercise 1
Intense Emotions
EARLY REJECTION

Each experience of rejection can have a great impact on our lives, especially if it occurred early in life. Through this exercise, you can re-experience an early feeling of rejection and discover how it has affected you.

Go Back in Time to When You Were Much Younger

Close your eyes and breathe deeply. Imagine that you are going inward and down until you take yourself gradually back to your childhood. Give yourself a few moments to recapture the feelings you had at that particular stage of life.

Locate an Incident of Early Rejection

The incident may or may not have occurred at the age you have gone back to, but more than likely it will have. If not, work with any incident that comes to mind. The rejection can be real or imagined. That is, someone might have verbally or physically rejected you in some way; or you may have simply felt that they were rejecting you. Work with either experience.

Replay the Incident in Your Imagination

Spend enough time to let all the details unfold, from start to finish.

- ✓ How old are you?
- ✓ Where are you?
- ✓ Who is with you?
- ✓ What is happening?

Focus on the Moment of Rejection

After you've replayed the incident completely, go back and focus only on the moment of rejection. Expand and amplify that moment as fully as you can. What happened specifically that caused you to feel rejected?

Locate in Your Body Where You Still Feel this Rejection

Scan through your body and find out exactly where you still feel this rejection.

- ✓ Is this feeling actually rejection? Could it be something else?
- ✓ What are the main characteristics of this body feeling?
- ✓ Does focusing on this spot recall other experiences with rejection?

Contemplate Your Relationship with Rejection

Ask yourself:

- ✓ How would I describe rejection? What is it?
- ✓ What is most difficult for me about feeling rejected?
- ✓ What have I learned from and about rejection?

Return Briefly to Your Early Incident

Spend a few moments thinking about the relationship of this early incident to your later life.

- ✓ What did I decide as a result of this early rejection?
- ✓ How did the incident shape my future?
- ✓ In what ways is this experience still affecting my life?

Open Your Eyes and Think for a Moment About Rejection

✓ How often in life do you feel rejected?

✓ Is rejection one feeling or a cluster of feelings?

✍ WRITING WARM-UP

✓ Make a list of other feelings you associate with rejection.

✓ In a paragraph, explain ways in which you sometimes feel rejected.

✍ WRITING ABOUT THE EXPERIENCE

✓ Write a journal entry in which you talk directly to the person who rejected you. Tell him or her exactly how you feel. After you finish, imagine that the person justifies his or her behavior. Write down what you imagine the person says to you in reply.

✓ Write a short essay that details your early rejection and explain how this experience has affected your concept of yourself and your life.

✓ Recall a time you worked to overcome the experience of rejection. Analyze the event and yourself: What was different about this rejection? How were you able to overcome it? What did you learn about rejection? Write an essay about this experience.

✍ EXPANDING THE EXPERIENCE

✓ Make a list of all the things you think the fear of rejection prevents you from doing. Share this list with two or three other classmates or friends and discuss among yourselves your fears of rejection. Plan ways for overcoming these fears. If you like, do some general reading on the concept of rejection and see if you can come up with any solutions. Then write an essay in which you explain what rejection is and how to overcome the fear of it. Use your own experiences as examples throughout the paper.

✓ Jump into the future. Imagine an event in which you expect to feel rejected. Visualize the event from start to finish and see yourself totally overcoming rejection. Dramatize the event in writing, using description and dialogue as if it is a scene in a movie. Show yourself victorious at the end.

Exercise 2
Intense Emotions

A THROW-IT-IN-THE-FIRE CONFESSION

Here's a chance to write down the one thing you've never confessed to another living soul. Or, if you told someone else about it, maybe you didn't tell the *whole* truth. Isn't there one important thing you left out? Didn't you change things around a bit? Don't worry—no one else will ever see this confession because you are going to throw it in the fire when you're through writing it.

Contemplate the Nature of Guilt and Confession

Take a few moments to put yourself into a state of reverie. Think in a general way about the nature of guilt and confession, of crimes against others. Think about things that others have done to you and things that you've done to others that you would call "terrible."

Mentally Examine Your Life

Pick out some of the things you've done that continue to cause you shame, guilt, or embarrassment. If you think through as much of your life as possible, some things will occur to you that you have long forgotten. You can make a list if you want to, but you don't have to write them down; simply run them through your mind.

Choose an Incident You Feel Comfortable Working With

When you feel ready, choose an incident to work with. Select an incident that does not upset you too much.

Recreate the Incident

Close your eyes and recreate the incident by thinking back through every step. Take time to breathe and travel back to the event.

- ✓ Locate the event in time and space.
- ✓ See all the other people involved.
- ✓ Observe yourself both physically and mentally as you were then.

Observe Yourself in Great Detail

Slowly go through all your actions and observe exactly what you felt, did, and thought throughout the event. Explore every part of what happened as fully as possible, especially the intentions and feelings behind your actions.

✓ What motivated you to take action?
✓ How did you feel immediately after?

Allow the Scene to Fade and Imagine Yourself Alone Seated Before a Fire

Before you open your eyes, shift the scene and imagine that you are seated next to a blazing fire, alone in a room at a desk. You are writing down your guilty moment in full detail. However, should anyone enter the room, you can immediately destroy this evidence by throwing it into the fire. Vividly see yourself beginning to write out your full confession.

✎ WRITING WARM-UP

✓ Complete this sentence: "In retrospect, I wish I had. . . . " Write as many additional sentences as necessary to complete your thoughts and feelings.

✓ Write down any action you feel you now could or want to take about this experience.

✎ WRITING ABOUT THE EXPERIENCE

✓ Write out your full confession. Be completely honest and include every detail. Write with the assurance that once you have confessed every detail of your "crime," you will burn it and no one else will ever know. Only you will finally know all the motives, thoughts, and feelings behind what you did. After you've fully written out your confession, you are free to destroy it. Nevertheless, you may find that through putting the event in writing, it has lost some of its emotional charge. You may decide to keep your written confession after all.

✎ EXPANDING THE EXPERIENCE

✓ Now write the story another way, telling it to a particular person in a confidential voice. How would the story change if you were telling it to your mother? Your best friend? An admissions committee at an elitist college? A jury? In deciding who your audience will be for this version, you will have to test boundaries to decide what's appropriate to include and what's appropriate to omit. If possible, see the movie *Rashomon* (created and directed by Akira Kurosawa) for an intense dramatization of how changeable "truth" is. Considered a masterpiece, this film portrays widely varying accounts of a murder reported by four different witnesses, including the murderer himself.

Intense Emotions 67

✓ Take your imagination for a ride and create a story in which a character does exactly what you did—and then, like you, writes out a confession before a blazing fire. However, just before he or she throws the confession into the fire, the phone rings and interrupts the process. As the character rushes to answer the phone, someone else comes along, picks up the confession, and reads it. Then what happens? Take the story from there and build it to a new climax.

Exercise 3
Intense Emotions
THE ANGRY EXERCISE

Anger, probably the least socially acceptable emotion, might also be the one least expressed. One of our strongest emotions, it's also the one that most often blocks other feelings. And we are unlikely to be in touch with our anger. Use this exercise to locate any anger you hold and either clear it out or accept it.

List All Your Major Angers

Keep asking yourself, "What makes my blood boil when I think about it?" until you get a full and complete list. In your head or written, include the following in your list:

✓ Things in general that make you angry, including irritations and annoyances
✓ Remembered old hurts and griefs
✓ Specific incidents in which you expressed your anger
✓ Specific incidents in which you did *not* express the anger you felt

Choose One of the Blood-Boilers from Your List to Work With

It doesn't have to be the biggest one—just the one you feel like working with right now. It can be a recent or not-so-recent incident, one in which you expressed your anger or did not. Just be certain to choose a specific event.

Review the Incident in Which You Felt Intense Anger

Close your eyes and take a few deep breaths. Then visualize the event:

✓ Where did it take place?
✓ Who or what triggered it?

- ✓ What happened?
- ✓ What had happened prior to the buildup of the anger?
- ✓ How did you handle your feelings before and after the incident?
- ✓ What was the final outcome?

Locate the Feeling of Anger in Your Body

With your eyes still closed, let the feeling grow as large as it wants to. Re-experience exactly how you feel when you are at the boiling point. Notice all your body changes. Now open your eyes and see how you feel.

See If You Have Any Unresolved Anger Left

If you still feel anger over the intense experience you just relived, stay in touch with that feeling until it begins to dissolve. Don't turn away from it or talk yourself out of it. If it doesn't dissolve, you might decide to hang onto it a bit longer. Give up your anger only when you're ready.

Let the Memory Dissolve and Check Into How You Feel About Anger

Give yourself some time to see how you feel about your current anger; then think objectively for a few minutes about how you handle anger in general—both your own and someone else's.

- ✓ What are your deepest feelings about anger?
- ✓ How do you act in the face of someone else's anger?
- ✓ How do you usually express your anger?

——————————■——————————

✐ WRITING WARM-UP

- ✓ In one paragraph, sum up your feelings about the emotion of anger. Is it good? bad? dangerous? useful? Make your statement strong and back up your opinion.

- ✓ In a journal entry, analyze how often and how well you handle your anger. Be as honest as possible.

✐ WRITING ABOUT THE EXPERIENCE

- ✓ Write about the moment of intense anger you re-experienced in the exercise, indicating exactly how you felt then and how you feel now about the experience. Describe your feelings as fully as possible. Include any insights about yourself that doing the exercise may have enabled. If you've experienced expressing your anger on the spot, compare how that feels to when you suppress anger.

✓ Describe a time when you were the target for someone else's anger. What happened? How did you feel? What did you do?

✍ EXPANDING THE EXPERIENCE

We've all witnessed the effects of unharnessed anger—wars, murders, assaults, mob violence, and severed relationships. Yet, when we constructively direct the powerful emotion of anger, we can create new possibilities. In the past few decades, the emotion of anger has received lots of attention. Many books have been written on analyzing, understanding, and handling it effectively, both personally and in groups, through conflict resolution. If you are interested in understanding more about anger, do some reading. You'll find many books—among them two short, comprehensive ones: *The Angry Book* by Theodore Isaac Rubin and *Anger: The Misunderstood Emotion* by Carol Tavris.

✓ Read about how you can constructively use feelings of anger. Then write an essay in which you explain the positive aspects of anger. Show the cause and effects of unexpressed anger and give specific information on how to use anger as a constructive emotion.

✓ Arrange for a group discussion of anger. Exchange ideas about different things that make you angry. Afterwards, choose one aspect of your world that makes you angry. Your subject can range from something as general as the high cost of dental care to something as specific to you as the pollution of a lake in your neighborhood that you can no longer use. Find out all you can about the problem. Then write a paper expressing your anger. Use a strong voice full of authority. You have a *right* to be angry about this subject. After you explain the problem, end your paper with your recommendations for solutions.

Exercise 4
Intense Emotions

JEALOUSY

Jealousy is another strong emotion we humans have to wrestle with. We call our feelings of intense rivalry with others envy when it's mild and jealousy when it's strong enough to make us miserable or out-of-control. Perhaps you have felt jealousy about a particular person over a long period of time; or perhaps you have felt momentary jealousy when someone else got something you wanted or deserved. This exercise will help you identify some moments of jealousy. As you begin to understand them, perhaps you will write some of them out of your system.

Close Your Eyes and Let the Word "Jealousy" and All Its Images Come to Mind

Breathe deeply as you think about jealousy:

✓ What other words do you associate with it?
✓ What scenes come to mind? The scenes can be from your own life, from movies, from books, or from your imagination.

Think Specifically About Jealousy Between Lovers

The most common—and probably the most dramatic—jealousy shows up in love relationships. Possessiveness, suspicion, infidelity—all familiar feelings for most of us.

✓ What scenes or stories about others come to mind?
✓ What personal experiences come to mind?

Consider Other Common Forms of Jealousy

Move your thinking now to other forms of jealousy, such as rivalry over sports, jobs, physical appearance, or financial success. Consider the many areas of life and activities that are apt to cause jealousy, especially for you.

Locate Several Instances of Your Own Feelings of Jealousy

Think back as far as early childhood to times when you felt jealous of another person.

✓ Do you see any common threads?
✓ Did you tell others about your jealousy?
✓ How did the feelings of jealousy cause you to act?

Now Focus on One Specific Incident in Which You Experienced Intense Jealousy

The incident can be a big one or a small one. Just try to remember the intensity of feeling surrounding it. Close your eyes and relive the event.

✓ Recall all the details of the incident.
✓ What specifically triggered your jealousy?

✓ Toward whom was your jealousy directed?
✓ See yourself in action: What did you do?

Recall all the Feelings Surrounding the Incident

Trace your feelings through the event, start to finish.

✓ What other feelings besides jealousy were present?
✓ Did anyone else know how you were feeling?
✓ What were the specific emotional qualities of your jealousy? Describe it fully.

Allow the Scene to Dissolve and Open Your Eyes

Reflect on the incident for a moment.

✓ Did your jealousy result in any benefits for you?
✓ What was the final outcome?

——■——

WRITING WARM-UP

✓ Write a brief analysis of yourself and jealousy. Were you surprised at your feelings during the exercise? What did you learn about yourself?

✓ Make a list of ten people you are jealous of and why. They don't have to be people you know personally.

WRITING ABOUT THE EXPERIENCE

✓ Narrate the experience you visualized above. Include your relationship with jealousy both then and now. If you learned anything new about yourself from the exercise, include that. Did your feelings of jealousy ultimately work for or against you?

✓ Jealousy is a natural human emotion that all of us feel from time to time. It's often a strong message for what we want for ourselves. One constructive use of jealousy is that we can analyze *why* we feel jealous, and then set out to acquire that entity for ourselves. Write about a time you used jealousy constructively.

EXPANDING THE EXPERIENCE

Because jealousy is so universal and intense, literature, plays, films, and popular songs use it as a constant theme. Two of the most powerful literary dramatizations of the extremes of jealousy are the Greek tragedy *Medea* by Euripedes and Shakespeare's *Othello*. A contemporary, more subtle study using jealousy as a pivotal force is John Knowles's book *A Separate Peace*, which examines the dangerous rivalry between close friends.

In an excerpt from the book, the scene is between the two major characters, Gene and Finny, seniors at a prep school in 1942, at the beginning of World War II. Gene is the first speaker and Finny the second:

"You wouldn't—" I wasn't sure I had the control to put this question—"mind if I wound up head of the class, would you?"

"Mind?" Two clear green-blue eyes looked at me. "Fat chance you've got, anyway, with Chet Douglass around."

"But you wouldn't mind, would you?" I repeated in a lower and more distinct voice.

He gave me that half-smile of his, which had won him a thousand conflicts. "I'd kill myself out of jealous envy."

—John Knowles
A Separate Peace

✓ Read a story, a play, or a novel in which jealousy is the pivotal emotion on which events turn. Write an analysis of the piece in which you examine the use of jealousy as a unifying theme. As much as possible, depend upon your own reading and observations; use outside sources only if absolutely necessary. The most important aspect of your paper will be for you to see with your own eyes how one intense emotion can give rise to a complicated story.

✓ For a shorter study, choose a song or poem about jealousy. Check out one of the old popular songs such as "Jalousie" (Gade-Bloom) or one of the newer, more chilling versions, such as "Every Breath You Take" by Sting. For a brilliant psychological portrait of consuming jealousy sketched in a few lines, read Robert Browning's poem "Soliloquy of the Spanish Cloister." Make your search fun. Look for numerous short pieces which dramatize jealousy. When you've found one that hooks you, study it word for word several times. Then write a paper in which you present the poem or song as a true-to-life portrait of jealousy in action.

✓ With a small group of friends, share your hidden jealousies. Take it slow and start with the ones you feel most safe in sharing. Choose one person as coordinator and compile a survey of actual jealousies that you come up with in the group. If possible, put the jealousies into specific categories and analyze them—how they are different, how they are alike, and so forth. Afterward, write a paper explaining what this group project taught you about yourself and others in relation to jealousy.

Chapter 8

OBSERVING YOUR LIFE

Remember yourself always and everywhere.

—Gurdjieff
Views from the Real World

Most of the exercises in this book are directed toward helping you unearth more knowledge about yourself. But the four exercises in this section specifically invite you, through self-observation, to add important meaning to some seemingly mundane events of your life. The following exercises will give you practice in observing—and remembering—yourself:

- *A Seven-Year Inventory*
- *A Parable for Living*
- *Fifteen Minutes Under the Microscope*
- *Your Life in Song*

Exercise 1
Observing
Your Life
A SEVEN-YEAR INVENTORY

The expression "seven-year itch" no doubt sprang from the fact that every seven years we shed our old skin and get a new one, and it has become a metaphor for the instinct to move on—to get out while we're ahead or before boredom strikes. Although we can't always meet this ideal, life still has a way of arranging events so that we experience a natural cycle of beginnings and endings. For this exercise, you'll do an inventory of your life for the past seven years—or for any seven-year interval. (You can instead use five, ten, or whatever other number feels natural to you.)

Trace One Interval in Your Life Through an Entire Cycle

Choose one interval in your life that covers seven (or any other number) years. Make a list of all the major events that took place during this period. Draw a graph to go with it if you like.

Close Your Eyes and Relive This Cycle

Relax and take several minutes to relive the cycle from beginning to end. You may have to think about it in detail to get the chronology straight. Run it through your mind like a movie, from start to finish, a couple of times.

Expand Each Important Event with Added Details

Look closely at each event. Take your time so that you clearly visualize each major event. See yourself in action and interacting with others:

✓ What do you look like?
✓ What are your major concerns?
✓ Which people are important in your life at each stage?
✓ What are your perceptions and feelings about each event?

Choose One of the Events from This Period and Relive It More Fully

Take one of the events you think is the most important and relive it in more detail. See how it fits into the seven-year cycle.

✓ How is it related to all the other events from this period?
✓ Why does it stand out?

Open Your Eyes and Complete the Inventory by Considering How Many of the Following Phases Are Apparent in Your Cycle

Break your cycle down into specific periods:

Initiation—The activity begins.

Flowering—You blossom and reap the benefits.

Pinnacle—You peak and have gone as far as you can.

Decline—The cycle starts down.

Transition—You move on and begin a new cycle.

———————■———————

✍ WRITING WARM-UP

✓ Draw a graph of the seven years, showing the peaks and valleys. Label each major event. At the bottom of the graph, write this sentence and complete it: "The major event that happened to me during this seven-year cycle was. . . ."

✓ In a few sentences, sum up this cycle in your life. Give your summary a title.

✍ WRITING ABOUT THE EXPERIENCE

✓ Put your inventory into a written narrative. Don't write just a sketchy outline. Rather, develop the narrative with specific details. As you write, new information might occur to you, so include that. Also include how closely your cycle resembles the five periods listed in the exercise. Conclude your narrative with a discussion of what you see as the major theme from this cycle.

✓ Looking back on this period of your life, what do you know now that would change the way you lived your life during those years? Write a journal entry exploring the road you *might* have taken but did not.

✍ EXPANDING THE EXPERIENCE

✓ Take the idea of the "other road" all the way. For inspiration, study Robert Frost's short classic poem, "The Road Not Taken," which vividly captures both the possibilities and the limitations of any choice we make. Think in detail about a specific choice you made and how your life might now be had you taken a different direction. Close your eyes and imagine yourself doing exactly opposite of what you did in reality. Let your imagination show you the chain of events that might have happened had you taken another turn. Then write a paper illustrating how, if you had taken that road, this is what would have happened. Write about this other life as if it were true. End your paper by expressing your thoughts and feelings about what actually happened and what could have happened.

✓ Arrange for a small group discussion with classmates. Have each person bring the inventory and explain it briefly. After the classmates have shared the inventories, let each person have a chance to discuss in more detail the event he or she thinks is the most significant and why. Later do some research into the seven-year itch idea, and the need for change. Or you might do some reading about life cycles. Then write an essay explaining your ideas and using your own cycles as an example throughout. Also include in detail a description of your most important event and explain its significance in relation to your cycle.

Exercise 2
Observing
Your Life

A PARABLE FOR LIVING

Most of the time we undertake routine activities mechanically, without paying attention to what we're doing. But every routine activity has embedded within it a lesson for living and offers us opportunities to break out of our ruts. Through closely observing yourself as you undertake regular daily activities, you can gain many new insights into yourself.

Choose One of Your Routine Activities

Pick something you do almost by remote control—washing the dishes, pruning a bush, welding a pipe, vacuuming a rug, typing a paper, folding clothes, eating dinner, driving your car, or taking a shower.

Perform the Activity in Your Usual Way or Close Your Eyes and Visualize Yourself Doing It

If possible, spend a few minutes doing the activity as usual. If it's not convenient to do the activity at this moment, mentally recreate it through visualizing yourself in action.

- ✓ What do you notice about the way you do the activity?
- ✓ What is happening internally as you do the external activity?
- ✓ What problems do you notice in getting the activity done?

Now Perform the Activity in a Slow, Meditative Way

This time, consciously slow down and put yourself into a different rhythm and frame of mind. Watch yourself as you perform the activity with the expectation that it will teach you something about yourself and how you live your life. Go through each step in slow motion.

Observe Yourself with New Eyes as You Do the Task

Watch yourself as you go through the usual motions and ask yourself:

- ✓ How do I feel as I'm doing this?
- ✓ How is my body responding?
- ✓ What am I thinking about?
- ✓ Am I giving this task my real attention? If not, where is it?
- ✓ Am I receptive to what the activity requires of me?

Put Yourself into Harmony with the Activity

Concentrate on the task that is before you. Adjust your tempo and the amount of energy you're using until you feel that your total attention is focused on the activity.

Open Up Your Awareness to the Lesson

As you continue to concentrate and observe yourself going through familiar motions, pay close attention to the feelings and attitudes that rise up within you. When you reach a point where you feel in harmony with the activity, open up to the lesson it has for you.

Ask yourself:

✓ What personal meaning is there in how I do this particular task?
✓ What can this activity teach me about myself?

———————■———————

✍ WRITING WARM-UP

✓ In a single sentence, state the lesson given to you through your slow-motion meditation.

✓ Make a list of all the ideas and images you can recall which came to you as you performed the activity.

✍ WRITING ABOUT THE EXPERIENCE

✓ Write a full account of your experience. Did observing yourself in the activity in any way change your method of working? Maybe you discovered many layers of action beneath this seemingly simple activity. If so, be certain to include a description of those actions. Also include the internal thoughts and feelings you had as you concentrated on the activity. End by explaining what the activity taught you through this process.

✓ If you have ever been a student of the martial arts (karate, kung fu, tai chi, aikido, judo, and so forth), you no doubt have experienced grounding yourself in inner meditation before beginning any practice or competition. If you've had such experience, write an essay about your involvement with a particular martial art, telling how the study of it has changed you in some way. If you haven't had the exact experience of studying a martial art, you can take some other activity or sport in which you've had practice in concentration and grounding, and write about that.

ANDING THE EXPERIENCE

been written about the value of using conscious awareness as a
...,prove performance in doing routine activities. Two books that in
1974 first popularized the idea of focused concentration are *The Inner Game
of Tennis* by W. Timothy Gallwey, a tennis coach, and *Zen and the Art of
Motorcycle Maintenance* by Robert M. Pirsig, a teacher and writer. Both books
expound the concept of becoming unified with the activity or object at .
hand.

Here is an excerpt from each book:

The ability to approach this state [of conscious awareness] is the goal of the
Inner Game. The development of inner skills is required, but it is interesting to
note that if, while learning tennis, you begin to learn control of the mind, to
concentrate the energy of awareness, you have learned something far more
valuable than how to hit a forceful backhand. The backhand can be used to
advantage only on a tennis court, but the skill of mastering the art of effortless
concentration is invaluable in whatever you set your mind to.

—W. Timothy Gallwey
The Inner Game of Tennis

So the thing to do when working on a motorcycle, as in any other task, is to
cultivate the peace of mind which does not separate one's self from one's surroundings. When that is done successfully then everything else follows naturally. Peace of mind produces right values, right values produce right thoughts.
Right thoughts produce right actions and right actions produce work which
will be a material reflection for others to see of the serenity at the center of
it all.

—Robert M. Pirsig
Zen and the Art of Motorcycle Maintenance

✓ Begin by writing a brief response to either of the two above ideas,
relating your response to what you learned in your own experiment
during the exercise. Later, read parts of either or both of the two
books and expand your essay to include new ideas you gained from
these books.

✓ Select an activity you enjoy and do well, such as chopping wood, playing a sport, dancing, sewing, or juggling. Check *Books in Print* and
magazine indexes to see some of the literature that's been written
about the activity. Select a few for study and read about the activity as
if you are a beginner and had no knowledge of it. After doing so, see
how the new knowledge (the mental) affects your performance of the
activity (the physical). Write a paper that includes the new information
you obtained as well as your experiences in observation and achieve-
ment after you conducted the study.

✓ With a group of friends or classmates, brainstorm about all the people you admire who have become experts in some activity. After the group effort, you can select, either as a group or individual project, an expert in a field of activity you're interested in: for example, Martha Graham on dancing, Leonard Bernstein on conducting, or Muhammad Ali on boxing. Read what the expert says about how he or she has learned to excel in the activity. Then write a report that details this person's philosophy and approach.

Exercise 3
Observing Your Life
FIFTEEN MINUTES UNDER THE MICROSCOPE

On the surface, this exercise is simple: You will examine yourself doing something that takes about 15 minutes. However, as you look closely at these 15 minutes, you will discover layers and layers of complexity—probably enough material to warrant a small novel.

Mentally Recount All the Things You Did Today or Yesterday

Think back over your day and mentally recount all the things you did. (You may go back to an earlier day, but choose a recent time.)

Pick One 15-Minute Segment from That Day

Choose one segment of your day in which you were doing something that took about 15 minutes. This activity can be as simple as taking a walk, cooking, or standing in line at the bank.

Close Your Eyes and Visually Recreate the Experience

Observe yourself in the action from start to finish. Take time to create a vivid mental picture of where you are and what you're doing.

Rerun the Event in Slow Motion

Go back and watch the whole experience again, this time in slow motion. Examine more closely what else was going on as you progressed through the 15 minutes.

✓ See each action as completely as possible.
✓ Pay attention to the transitions between actions: What prods you to finish one action and begin another?

Observing Your Life 81

✓ Notice what else is going on around you that is outside your frame of reference but which you still observe.

✓ Tune in to how your body feels.

Now Rerun the Sequence a Third Time and Recollect What You Were Thinking

Go back through each movement once again. This time, trace every thought you're aware of as you undertake the different actions. You now have a dual mental screen—one for your external actions and one for your internal thoughts.

Slow Down Time Even Further

Slow down time until you are looking at each mental and physical event as if it took much longer to transpire than it actually did. Mentally record every turn of thought and feeling that you can remember. You may have to rerun the scene several times in your mind's eye in order to uncover everything. Continue until you have examined these 15 minutes as closely as if they were under a microscope.

✐ WRITING WARM-UP

✓ Write several sentences describing how the process of the exercise affected you. Were you able to go back and trace your thoughts? Did you discover anything you thought you had forgotten?

✓ In your journal, draw a line down the middle of the page. On the left side, write down a list of the sequence of external events—what you actually did during those 15 minutes. Don't leave out anything. On the right side, write down a sequential list of the internal events—all of your thoughts in the order in which they occurred.

✐ WRITING ABOUT THE EXPERIENCE

✓ Write a full description of the 15-minute episode, giving both the external and the internal events. Get down every single thing you remembered. End by explaining what it was like for you to examine 15 minutes in such detail and tell what you learned about yourself and your thought processes.

✓ Choose *one* of the mental activities from the 15 minutes—a thought, a memory, or an image, for example—and examine it in closer detail. Follow the thread all the way and let it write its own story. See where it will lead you. If you find your imagination taking over completely, that's fine.

✍ EXPANDING THE EXPERIENCE

In this exercise, you got a taste of a literary technique called "stream-of-consciousness," a term the American philosopher/psychologist William James created in 1890 in his book *The Principles of Psychology*. James set forth the concept that our thoughts, memories, and impressions are fluid, like a stream, rather than fixed. Around this same period, Henri Bergson, the French philosopher, came to a similar conclusion about time. He believed that time was not linear, and that people experience time as a continuous flow, going back and forth from past to present. These two ideas became the basis for experimental fiction where writers employed stream-of-consciousness techniques to present their characters' feelings, thoughts, reactions, and memories. Most modern writers regularly use these techniques now.

✓ If you are interested in this concept, undertake a deeper study of stream-of-consciousness—either as a literary device or as a psychological theory. If you're interested in the theoretical ideas, study first-hand the works of James and Bergson. If you're interested in the literary ideas, study some major writers who first used stream-of-consciousness, such as James Joyce, Virginia Woolf, William Faulkner, or Dorothy Richardson. Much critical material is now available on this subject. One short, excellent book is *Stream of Consciousness in the Modern Novel* by Robert Humphrey. Since this study will be broad, you will have to decide with your teacher's help what kind of paper you want to produce as a result of your research. If you're interested in writing fiction, here is an opportunity for you to experiment with your own stream-of-consciousness writing.

✓ You've had the experience of recalling all of your thoughts from a past 15-minute segment. Now you can have the experience in the present. With one or two classmates or friends, set up the experiment ahead of time. Find a place where you won't be distracted—perhaps the classroom. Set a clock or timer for 15 minutes and for the entire time, write down every single thought that comes to your mind. If you closely follow the process, your hand will not be able to keep up with all of your thoughts; but do your best. Don't try to control your thoughts—just follow them around and see where they lead you. Once the 15 minutes are up, have all the group read parts of what they've written. After the reading, discuss the whole process and see what you discovered. Later you can write up a report—either group or individual—giving details of the experiment and explaining what you learned first-hand about stream-of-consciousness. Include what you've written as part of the report.

YOUR LIFE IN SONG

Songs of love. Songs to dance to. Songs on the radio, in the elevator, at the bank. Songs everywhere. Hardly any crevice of life is not touched by popular song sometime, somewhere. And hardly any year of your life is not intertwined with songs.

Think in General About Yourself in Relation to Popular Songs

✓ Do you keep up with the latest songs?
✓ Do you feel current songs are better or worse than those of earlier years?
✓ Where do you most often listen to music?

Write Down a List of Your Favorite Songs

As rapidly as possible, make a random list of all the songs that you love, both past and present. After you've made the list, go back and indicate the year and even the specific month, if possible, with which you associate the song.

Close Your Eyes and Remember a Song You Loved Early in Life

If you've always been crazy about music, you might have learned to sing before you learned to talk. Take some time now to breathe, relax, and travel slowly back in time. Visualize yourself at an early age and see yourself listening to or singing a song that you loved.

✓ How old are you?
✓ What do you look like?
✓ Where are you listening to the music? By what method?
✓ What do you associate the song with at this time?
✓ What do you love most about this song?

Now Travel from This Earliest Memory Back Up Through Your Life

Keep your eyes closed and come slowly back up through your life to the present. Take a good bit of time with this. Run through each year of your life and see which songs you associate with your life, year by year. There may be many songs for some years and none for others. Remember yourself listening to specific songs in specific places.

Choose One of the Songs to Examine More Closely

Pick one of the songs you remembered and go further with it.

- ✓ When was this song popular?
- ✓ When was it important to you?
- ✓ What memory do you associate it with?
- ✓ Was the song important at other times during your life?

Examine the Music and the Lyrics

Now hear the song. Recapture the music and as many of the lyrics as you can remember.

- ✓ What is the basic message of the lyrics?
- ✓ How is the music put together? What stands out about it?
- ✓ If there is more than one version of the song, think about the other versions and how they compare to your favorite one.

Zero In on One Important Moment You Associate with This Song

Imagine yourself in the center of this song, feeling its effect on you. Think about one important moment when you heard this song:

- ✓ How old are you? What is going on in your life at this time?
- ✓ Who else is with you?
- ✓ What are you doing? See yourself as vividly as possible.
- ✓ Why is this moment important?
- ✓ What does the song contribute to this moment?

Now Open Your Eyes and Reflect on the Information You Just Obtained

Mentally run back through the experience of reliving your life through song.

- ✓ What stands out most for you about yourself in relation to songs?
- ✓ Which memory was strongest for you?

✍ COMPLETING THE EXPERIENCE

- ✓ Write down all the lyrics you can remember from the last song you visualized in the exercise. Add a summary statement which explains what you think the lyrics mean and what relationship they have to your life.

✓ What is the very first song you remember loving? Give the title of the song and describe your attachment to it.

✎ WRITING ABOUT THE EXPERIENCE

✓ Describe the most important moment connected with a song from the exercise. Be sure to include specific details and explain what contribution the song made to this moment. Include some of the significant lyrics. End your essay with a couple of retrospective paragraphs in which you explain why this song and this memory still stand out in your mind. What meaning does this memory have for your life now?

✓ Analyze your life through songs. Recollect the experience of the exercise in which you went year by year through your life. In what ways did particular song titles or their lyrics seem to summarize different phases of your life?

✎ EXPANDING THE EXPERIENCE

The popular tunes of today eventually become the classics of tomorrow. It wasn't too long ago that the waltz was considered naughty; now it's thought to be stuffy. Elvis Presley gyrating to "Hound Dog" was trash and nonsense once upon a time. Now it's sentimental memorabilia—the good ole days when songs had umph. Back when the Beatles first hit the radio with "I Wanna Hold Your Hand," parents were screaming, "You call that music?" But less than a decade later, symphony orchestras were playing elaborate versions of Beatle songs. You see the drift. You've probably already lived long enough to see music in transition—from intellectual rock to hard rock to soft rock to rock and roll to rap and so on.

Two excellent sources for looking further at the development of popular song are

American Popular Song by Alec Wilder, which traces the history of song writing in America from 1885 to 1950 and covers important song writers such as George Gershwin, Cole Porter, and Hoagy Charmichael.

The Rolling Stone Illustrated History of Rock and Roll, which traces, through both text and photographs, the earliest beginnings (both in America and England) of rock in the rural South in the 1920s and ends with the rock artists of the late 1970s (such as Steely Dan and Bruce Springsteen.) The book offers detailed discographies on every important performer of rock, rock and roll, soul, and rhythm and blues. A later publication, *The Rolling Stone Encyclopedia of Rock & Roll,* offers brief essays and short discographies of over 1,300 groups and individuals from Abba to ZZ Top.

✓ With a group of friends or classmates, have some fun discussing the songs you came up with in the exercise. Then move to a discussion of *one* particular strain of music that interests you as a group, such as jazz, rap, blues, reggae, or punk rock. After the discussion gives you some ideas and information, undertake a study of the development of one type of music. Make an outline of all you think is important to cover and then make one person responsible for collecting information on each topic. If possible, make an audiovisual presentation of your findings, or at least an audiotape giving segments of the most important songs. In your report, emphasize the contributions this particular music has made to the development of music in general. If a group project doesn't work out, you can do your own research and write a paper that traces the development of one particular type of music.

✓ Choose one composer of popular song—someone who writes both lyrics and music. Choose a contemporary figure (such as Stevie Wonder, Kate Bush, or Laura Nyro) or an earlier composer (such as Cole Porter or Hank Williams). Do a survey of the composer's music and find some information about how he or she works as a composer. Then write a paper which describes and illustrates the composer's musical development. (You can instead choose a collaborative team such as Elton John/Bernie Taupin or Darrell Hall/John Oates and discuss their development as collaborators.)

✓ Have some more fun. Do a paper on song trivia—sort of a musical scavenger hunt. Find a central theme which interests you. For example, censorship of songs: Find out why "Gloomy Sunday" and "Junko Partner" were banned from the radio in the 1940s and how today's rap music avoids being banned. Find out the history of patriotic war songs. Learn about songs that were flip sides and later became hits. The possibilities are endless.

Part III

THE OUTER WORLD

The outer world is an extension of the inner world. What we see when we look out is colored by what is inside. Sometimes we feel connected to what we see—even merged with it; other times we feel alienated and separated. Both experiences are useful to us in different ways. To become aware of both the inner and the outer worlds simultaneously is to interlace our observations of the world with an inner awareness that gives clarity and meaning to our daily lives.

Chapter 9

——— SEEING ———

In this twentieth century, to stop rushing around, to sit quietly on the grass, to switch off the world and come back to the earth, to allow the eye to see a willow, a bush, a cloud, a leaf, is an unforgettable experience.

—Frederick Franck
The Zen of Seeing

The old saying, "Whatever is before you is your teacher," is full of truth. Yet in order to learn the lesson that is before you, you have to first learn to see on many levels—and with more than your eyes. In these exercises, you will have the chance to expand all five of your senses and develop new ways of perceiving things below the surface. The section includes the following exercises:

- *The Eye of the Camera*
- *Here-and-Now*
- *A Rock*
- *A Kitchen Utensil*

Exercise 1
Seeing THE EYE OF THE CAMERA

Our eyes record thousands of scenes each day, though we usually don't notice all we take in. This is a visual exercise in which you use your eyes like a camera to record instant photos of simple things you might normally overlook. You'll be closing and opening your eyes throughout the exercise, so read the instructions all the way through ahead of time. Or, if possible, have your teacher or a friend count you through the exercise.

Relax Your Eyes Through This Simple Exercise

Before beginning the exercise, relax your eyes by stretching them as you would your arms and legs.

✓ Look first to the right, then to the left several times.
✓ Roll your eyes in a circle from right to left and then left to right.
✓ Look up, then down.
✓ Rub your hands briskly together until you feel heat accumulating, then close your eyes and cup your palms over them, allowing the warmth to penetrate your eyes.

Open Your Eyes and Prepare for the Exercise

Consciously relax your eyes and fix your gaze on some object or point nearby. Take in what you see.

Close Your Eyes and Begin the Sequence of Opening and Closing Them

✓ Close your eyes and count slowly 1–2–3. On the count of three open your eyes again.
✓ Mentally record what you see, just as a camera lens would do. Don't reach for the scene with your eyes—just allow it to come to you.
✓ Now let the shutter click by closing your eyes. While you count slowly 1–2–3, watch the scene that you just recorded develop on the screen of your inner vision.

Turn Your Head in Another Direction and Repeat the Action

With your eyes closed, turn your head so your line of vision is directed elsewhere and to the count of one, two, three, repeat the process of opening and then closing your eyes. Don't shift your gaze and look for a scene you like better. Keep your gaze where it lands and click the shutter.

Repeat the Action Several Times

Continue the action of closing your eyes, turning your head, and opening and closing your eyes again. Do this six to eight times, keeping the rhythm of one, two, three. You probably won't remember everything you see and that's fine. Yet without any big effort on your part, your eyes will have recorded several scenes that you'll remember when you start to write.

———————————■———————————

✍ WRITING WARM-UP

✓ Think for a moment about all the things you saw. Then make a quick list of everything you remember seeing. After you've finished, go back

92 *Seeing / The Eye of the Camera*

and add brief notations to each scene as to the colors, shapes, and unusual qualities that you saw.

✓ Describe in a few sentences how the experience of using your eyes in this way affected you. In what ways did things look different to you? How did your eyes feel?

✍ WRITING ABOUT THE EXPERIENCE

✓ Write a short paper in which you describe all the things you observed. Include also your observations about how it feels to use your eyes in this manner.

✓ Write a full description of the one detail you saw which was the most vivid for you. Recreate the scene from your memory and make it as long and detailed as possible. Add a drawing of it if you want to. The point is to turn a three-second observation into a description of a few hundred words. Make the object or scene live through your description. Once you've completed the description, let your imagination take over and lead you to a full ending.

✍ EXPANDING THE EXPERIENCE

If you enjoyed using your eyes in this way, you might like to explore this way of seeing further. The quotation which introduces this section comes from an inspiring book, *The Zen of Seeing,* by Frederick Franck. Franck believes there is a way of seeing where "the split between the seer and what is seen is obliterated." He teaches Seeing/Drawing "as a way of meditation, a way of getting into intimate touch with the visible world around us, and through it . . . with ourselves."

✓ Read Franck's book and try some of the techniques for Seeing/Drawing in it. Then write a paper explaining the process—how it is done—and what you discovered about it from your own experience. Include some of your drawings as examples.

Another way of looking at the world and art is set forth by John Berger and others in *Ways of Seeing.* Berger says: "Seeing comes before words. The child looks and recognizes before it can speak." The premise of the book is that we choose what we will see and that what we choose to see is affected by who we are at any given moment:

We never look at just one thing; we are always looking at the relation between things and ourselves. Our vision is continually active, continually moving, continually holding things in a circle around itself, constituting what is present to us as we are.

—John Berger
Ways of Seeing

Seeing 93

✓ Locate Berger's short, beautifully illustrated book and follow his directions for looking at some of the illustrations of works of art. Then write a paper which presents one of the major ideas from the book and back up your points with illustrations from your own experience about what worked for you and what did not work.

Exercise 2
Seeing
HERE-AND-NOW

We're always hearing about how important it is to be in the moment, to "be here now." But it's not always that easy to do. This exercise will help you focus your five senses on the present and open up to what's around you—connecting with one or more of your senses will always bring you immediately into the present moment.

Fix Your Attention on Each of Your Five Senses

Think for a moment about each of the five senses and the organs primarily responsible for that sense. Spend a few moments thinking about each of them.

✓ Eyes—Sight (What do you see?)
✓ Ears—Hearing (What do you hear?)
✓ Nose—Smell (What do you smell?)
✓ Mouth—Taste (What do you taste?)
✓ Skin—Touch (What do you feel?)

Observe What You See

Turn off your mental judgments and ideas and just observe what you see. Your eyes will take in many sights without effort. Write down several things that you see—as specifically as possible.

Observe What You Hear

If you simply relax and allow your hearing to expand, many different sounds will come to you. Try to describe the sounds at the moment you're hearing them.

Observe What You Smell

Breathe deeply through your nose to see what smells come easily to you. Start with these, then consciously choose different objects to smell and describe. Choose objects you might not normally smell—wood, paper, leather.

Observe What You Taste

You'll have to choose items to taste—but they don't all have to be food. You might try out old familiars such as a pretzel, an apple, or sparkling water. Try to write about them at the moment you're tasting them. You can also try out the tip of your ballpoint pen, a flower, a piece of paper, or other things babies routinely put into their mouths.

Observe What You Touch

Use your fingers and hands to feel the shapes and textures of different objects around you—corduroy, a piece of pottery. In addition, become aware of how the air feels on your skin and the way your clothes feel against your body.

✐ WRITING WARM-UP

✓ Write a paragraph about how the experience was for you. How do you feel about your powers of observation? What did you notice about yourself?

✐ WRITING ABOUT THE EXPERIENCE

✓ Write three sentences for each of the five senses, for a total of 15 sentences. Don't struggle to be clever; just write down as simply as possible what your senses perceived. Use present tense as if the experience is happening right now, and locate your descriptions in time and space when you can.

Examples:

I see a man in overalls and a red cap swatting a fly off a gasoline pump.

I hear the soft plunk of big raindrops on the windshield of the car.

I smell the rancid odor of tarnished metal on the knife.

I taste glue on my tongue as I lick the stamp.

I feel the cold ceramic of the cup against my forehead.

✓ Take one of your sentences and expand it into several paragraphs, adding as many other specific details as you observed and then filling in the rest with your imagination. Turn the observation into a short scene.

Examples:

I see a man in overalls and a red cap swatting a fly off a gasoline pump. The fly obviously won't go away because now the man has grabbed a rag and is reaching way up in the air trying to hit the fly. He's forgotten all about the customers waiting for gas. . . .

I hear the soft plunk of big raindrops as they hit the windshield of the car. I lie across the front seat and close my eyes and wait for my friends to return from the video store. All of a sudden the rain starts to come down very hard. . . .

✑ EXPANDING THE EXPERIENCE

✓ Take one of the senses and write a memory of it—for example, "A Memory of Smell," "A Memory of Sound." In your paper, take a specific moment in which one of the five senses played a major part, describe the moment, and then explain why this memory is still so important to you.

✓ The term "sensory awareness" has become an everyday phrase primarily through the work of one woman, Charlotte Selver, who has been teaching sensory training for almost half a century. Locate the book based on her work, *Sensory Awareness*, written by her husband, Charles Brooks. The book explains the philosophy and value of training the senses and then gives numerous exercises for doing so— employing the senses in a variety of activities such as yawning, stretching, sitting, tasting, speaking, and so forth. Read several chapters in the book and do some of the exercises, either alone or with a group of friends with one person at a time acting as the leader. Afterward, write a paper explaining what sensory awareness is and what you learned about it and yourself through the exercises.

Exercise 3 $\underline{\hspace{2cm}}$ A ROCK
Seeing

A rock—a hard piece of the earth's crust—something we step on, kick, and curse, is also a thing of beauty which we often stop to admire and collect. Because rocks literally support the very ground we walk upon, they can offer us special knowledge of the earth and our connection to it. If you have a rock collection, that's a perfect place to choose one for the meditation. If not, take a walk outdoors to find a rock for the following meditation.

Choose a Rock from a Group of Others

Pick a rock, and notice your thoughts as you make your selection. Ask yourself these questions:

✓ Why am I choosing this particular rock?
✓ Is this the one I really want? (Be sure not to settle for one you don't care for.)

Place the Rock in the Palm of Your Hand

Look closely at your rock and take in all its features.

✓ Look at the shape of it.
✓ Test the weight and feel of it in your hand.

Examine the Rock from Every Angle

Turn the rock over and all around until you have seen it from every angle and have taken in all the variety that it offers. Really see all the unique details of this rock.

Consider the Rock as a Piece of Nature

✓ What are the natural properties of a rock?
✓ What function does a rock serve?
✓ What other representations of nature do you see in the rock?

Establish a Relationship with Your Rock

Spend a few moments with the rock until you feel a connection with it. In some way, see the rock as an extension of yourself. Does holding the rock in your hand change the way you feel either physically or mentally? Ask yourself:

✓ What attracts me to this rock?
✓ How is this rock like myself? Are there any characteristics we share?
✓ What can this rock teach me?

———————■———————

✍ WRITING WARM-UP

✓ Before you begin to write, spend a few moments with your attention focused on the rock, remembering the process you just went through. Then, with your rock next to you, make rapid notes about anything that comes to your mind.

✓ Place the rock on your notebook or journal (or a piece of paper) and draw an outline of it. Indicate with shadings the areas that seem most important to you. Label the important parts.

✍ WRITING ABOUT THE EXPERIENCE

✓ Write a detailed account of what went on inside of you as you did the exercise. What aspects of yourself did you see in the rock?

✓ Write a lighthearted fantasy in which you invite your rock to speak to you and tell you important things you need to know about yourself and the world.

✓ Using this same exercise, choose another object from nature—such as a seashell, a flower, a piece of fruit, a nut—and observe it closely. Then write a paper about it and compare this experience with the one you had with the rock. In what ways are the two objects alike? Different?

✍ EXPANDING THE EXPERIENCE

The ancient philosophy of Zen which originated in Japan has gradually become intertwined in the western world and you can now find many books with *Zen* as part of the title. The Zen idea that there is one single meaning in life which is expressed in every single variation is the basis for this exercise on the rock. Practice in seeing this oneness in all its forms can teach us much about ourselves and our lives. The following Japanese *haiku* perfectly expresses this idea:

> POTATO
> Inside of one potato
> there are mountains and rivers.
> —Shinkichi Takahashi
> *Translated by Harold P. Wright*

✓ Read more about Zen philosophy, concentrating on how this philosophy has been expressed in art and poetry. A good book to start with is *Zen: Direct Pointing to Reality* by Anne Bancroft, which briefly explains Zen influence in poetry, landscape, the martial arts, and so forth. The book is liberally illustrated and contains a good bibliography which will lead you to further sources. Part of the book is based on the teachings of Shunryu Suzuki and his book, *Zen Mind, Beginner's Mind.* Suzuki was a famous Zen master who came to America in the late 1950s and established the first Zen monastery in this country. After you have gained some understanding of the Zen philosophy, put together a paper on how Zen has influenced art and poetry. Collect samples and include them in your paper. If possible, include your own experience with the rock and/or other objects as further example of what you have learned about the concept of Zen oneness.

✓ The Native Americans hold all of nature in reverence and believe that every expression of nature—rocks, trees, rain, rivers, and so forth—contains a deity within it. Find out more about the Native Americans' beliefs about nature. Explain some of their rituals that revolve around the sacredness of nature and the four elements. In addition to reading materials, you might locate documentaries and may even find people to interview. Focus on the contrast between the Native Americans' view of nature and the average American's view. Write a paper showing the differences.

✓ Choose some aspect of nature which interests you and find out all you can about it. This can be a large piece of nature, such as mountains, caves, or lakes; or it can be a small piece, such as rocks, flowers, or moss. Study the practical aspects of this part of nature: How is it formed? Why is it necessary? What specific contributions does it make to life on earth? Once you have explained the practical aspects, you might want to end your paper by pointing out some of the imaginative, symbolic qualities. What other meaning, beyond the practical, does this part of nature carry?

Exercise 4
Seeing **A KITCHEN UTENSIL**

Every day we use and depend upon objects which we seldom look at. Take, for example, kitchen utensils. They may seem to be mundane, but many of them, when looked at closely, can be as engaging as a work of art.

Choose a Kitchen Utensil to Work With

Choose a utensil that has some aesthetic appeal to you—it can be one you use regularly or one you've never used. An interesting experiment, in fact, is to work with a utensil that you know little about.

Place the Utensil in Front of You on a Table and Look at It Objectively

Take an objective look at the utensil. Turn it around and look at it from all sides. Forget what you know about this object and mentally record what you actually see. Don't rush. Take several minutes to study it.

✓ What are some of its features?
✓ What comes to mind when you look at it?

Pick It Up and Get the Feel of It

Hold the utensil.

✓ What kind of material is it composed of?
✓ How does it feel to the touch?

Look at the Way It Is Put Together

Think about how the utensil was made.

- ✓ Would manufacturing it be simple or complex?
- ✓ How do you envision it being manufactured?
- ✓ What are some of its unusual parts?

Reflect on Its Origin

Think about how it came into being.

- ✓ What was used in its place before it was invented?
- ✓ Who invented it?
- ✓ What country does it come from?

Think About the Value of This Utensil

Consider the purpose of the utensil.

- ✓ How is it used?
- ✓ What need does it fill?
- ✓ What gap would it leave if it disappeared from use?

———————■———————

✍ WRITING WARM-UP

- ✓ Look at the utensil and, keeping your eyes on it the whole time, draw what you see.

- ✓ In one paragraph, describe the utensil.

✍ WRITING ABOUT THE EXPERIENCE

- ✓ Take some of the sentences you wrote in the above paragraph and set them up in the form of a poem. Add or subtract lines until you have made a poem which describes the utensil. Title your poem the name of the utensil—Grater, Teaball, Peeler—but don't mention the name of the utensil in the poem itself. Use the poem to describe the utensil as you see it.

- ✓ Write a full description of the utensil, giving each part a separate paragraph. Describe it in complete detail so that someone who has never seen one before can understand what it looks like and how it functions. After you give a concrete description of the utensil, speculate on how it was invented and the need it fills.

✍ EXPANDING THE EXPERIENCE

Choose an object that interests you—perhaps something you use every day. The object can be functional such as hair dryers, clocks, chairs or something aesthetic such as vases, wind chimes, necklaces. Use some of the ideas and questions in the exercise first to study the object more closely. Then track down information on the object. Search especially for illustrations which show how it has changed over time. Keep these questions in mind:

✓ How did the object originate?
✓ If it was originally functional, when and how did it become ornamental and aesthetic?
✓ What is the contrast between its earliest form and its current form?

✓ Write an illustrated paper which explains the origin of the object and which illustrates the stages of development. You can work from past to present or present to past—that is, begin with the form it is in now and then trace it back to its beginnings. Be certain to acknowledge the source for all of your illustrations and to use captions which make clear the purpose of each illustration.

✓ With a group of friends or classmates, discuss a number of objects which have significance for other people but which you know little about—for example the *yarmulke* worn by Jewish men or the rosary beads carried by nuns. Choose one of the objects which interests you—either as a solo project or with the group. Find out about the object through both reading and personal interviews with someone you know who uses the object. Write a paper explaining what the object is, how it evolved, and why it is significant to a particular group of people. Use illustrations when you can.

Chapter 10

—————— PEOPLE ——————

The thing to wait on, to reach there in time for, is the moment in which people reveal themselves. You have to be ready, in yourself; you have to know the moment when you see it.

—Eudora Welty
The Eye of the Story

In a world filled with other human faces, we often see only ghosts of our own face parading continuously in front of our eyes. Caught in the spell of our own feelings and judgments, we often miss the spectacle before us, the richness available to us in truly seeing other people as they dance in and out of our lives. Here are four exercises to help you practice the art of seeing other people.

- *People-Watching*
- *Outrageous Acts*
- *A Family Legend*
- *The Other*

Exercise 1
People
PEOPLE-WATCHING

Each person you see could be the central character in a novel—each of them could tell you a book about himself or herself. The fine art of people-watching will provide you with insights into human nature. It can also give you many new characters for your own writing.

Go to a Public Place Where You Can Sit Without Interruption

Go to a public place—such as a shopping mall, the college union, a train station or airport, a library—any place where you can sit for 30 minutes without interruption. Before beginning, pause, breathe, and relax so that you are in a meditative state of mind.

Sit and Observe the People Around You

Put your judgments aside and simply look at people as they come and go. Keep at it for at least 30 minutes. Take brief notes if you like, but don't get caught up in writing too much. Keep your attention on your observations.

Watch the People in Action

Look at how people act—how they walk, talk, and so forth. Notice any unusual behavior or mannerisms.

Think About What You See

- ✓ How are people alike?
- ✓ How are they different?
- ✓ What are some of the most obvious characteristics you observe in different people?
- ✓ What are some of the more subtle characteristics?
- ✓ What do many of these people seem to want?

Zero In on One Person Who Captures Your Imagination

Think about why this person appeals to you.

- ✓ What are some of the characteristics that attract you?
- ✓ Does this person remind you of others you know?
- ✓ Can you see that person as a character in a play or story? If so, in what role?

Notice Your Own Thoughts and Emotions

Tune into yourself as you sit there observing:

- ✓ How do you feel when you're just observing rather than making judgments?
- ✓ How do certain people trigger specific feelings in you—such as anger, love, disapproval, pity, envy, pleasure?
- ✓ Which people brought up prejudices in you?

✍ WRITING WARM-UP

- ✓ Make a list of all the people you observed, giving a brief description of each.

✓ Write a full description of the one person who most caught your attention. Explain what fascinated you about this person.

✍ WRITING ABOUT THE EXPERIENCE

✓ Write a paper based on your observations. Tell what you saw and how it affected you: Include brief character sketches of the people who most attracted your interest. Explain what you discovered about people in general.

✓ Write an analysis of yourself as an observer of people. What did you discover about yourself? In what ways did you see your own self reflected in others?

✍ EXPANDING THE EXPERIENCE

✓ Think of a human trait which puzzles or bothers you the most and set out to learn everything you can about it. Read about this trait from several different perspectives: psychological, sociological, historical, and so forth. After you've done balanced research, write an essay which first describes the trait and then analyzes the causes behind this trait. Use examples from your own experience or observation to support your point of view.

✓ Arrange a "people" talk with several other classmates or friends. Have some fun discussing all the human quirks which puzzle or bother you the most. During the course of the discussion, think of specific people you know who demonstrate some of these quirks and characteristics. Then brainstorm for outstanding characters from novels (use novels because they are long enough to develop the character more fully). Choose a character who demonstrates a certain trait that you feel strongly about—it can be one that you would like to have yourself or one that bothers you. Read the novel closely, taking notes and marking spots that you think prove your idea. Then write a paper which sets forth your opinion and back up your opinion with specific references to the book.

Exercise 2
People
OUTRAGEOUS ACTS

Some people can get away with more than should be legal. Surely you know a few people like that—maybe you're even one of them. Certainly literature is full of them. Wherever we encounter these people, we're bound to shake our heads in wonder at how they pull off their outrageous acts. "Outrageous" used in this sense means outlandish, beyond what is expected or socially acceptable. Keep it light for this exercise.

Spend Some Time Running Through All the Outrageous Acts You Can Remember Witnessing

Think of funny, amazing, or zany things you've seen people do. Stretch your mind and go for the most outrageous act you can think of. This may take a little time. Make a list if that helps. If you can't think of any you remember seeing, jot down some acts other people have told you about. Maybe you saw an outrageous act on TV or read about it in the news. Maybe you participated in it yourself.

Think About the Motivation Behind Such Acts

Spend some time thinking about human nature in general and what prompts unusual behavior.

✓ What kind of people usually do outrageous acts?
✓ What, in general, motivates them?

Use One of the Acts on Your List to Analyze

If you actually saw an outrageous event happen or if you took part in it yourself, recount it in your imagination. If you only heard about it, envision it happening in your mind. Close your eyes and visualize it.

✓ Locate it in time and place.
✓ Who are all the characters involved?
✓ What kind of person committed the outrageous act?
✓ What action took place prior to this?

Examine the Outrageous Act in Detail

Zero in on just the outrageous action itself.

✓ In what specific ways did this action differ from what is usually expected?
✓ What do you think motivated the person to do it?
✓ In what ways was it justified? Did the situation merit it?
✓ In what ways was it truly "outrageous"?
✓ What was the final outcome?
✓ What was the effect on others?

———————■———————

106 *People / Outrageous Acts*

✍ WRITING WARM-UP

✓ Make a list of all the outrageous acts you can think of. Put a star by the ones you like the most. Then circle the best one on your list and write a couple of sentences that describe it.

✓ Write a secret journal entry about your own outrageous acts—both the real and the imagined.

✍ WRITING ABOUT THE EXPERIENCE

✓ Imagine the outrageous act you visualized in the exercise as a scene in a movie or a book. Write a narrative account of it in detail, building up to the outrageous act as a climactic moment. Your job is to make it seem as outrageous as possible, so don't just tell what happened; *show* it.

✓ Write about a time when you acted outrageously in some way—perhaps you acted without thinking or took some action that was unexpected or extreme. What resulted from this experience? How did you feel about it at the time? How do you feel about it in retrospect?

✓ Write a character sketch about the most outrageous person you have ever known. Give anecdotes that illustrate the ongoing outrageous nature of this person.

✍ EXPANDING THE EXPERIENCE

✓ Spend some time with a group of friends or classmates exchanging stories about some of the outrageous acts you've either heard about or witnessed. After all the stories have been told, choose one that you heard about from the group (rather than one you witnessed) and write up an account of the event from memory. Don't check the details until after you have written your own story. When the group meets again, read your stories aloud and check them for accuracy. How much of your story was real and how much of it was filled in through your imagination?

✓ Imaginative literature supplies us with a wealth of characters who do outrageous things. That's part of why we read: to see people doing all those wild things we only daydream about. Put together another discussion group and this time brainstorm about some of the outrageous acts you remember from novels, short stories, plays, or movies. Remember, these should not be evil or harmful acts but rather acts that show some unusual quirk of character. After the discussion, read several of the pieces of literature (or see the movies) which caught your interest. Then write a paper that describes a number of these outrageous acts. Try to find a common theme or some type of similarity among the acts and organize your paper around this central idea.

Exercise 3
People

A FAMILY LEGEND

We tend to take our own families for granted—tend to think of the members in our family as just ordinary people. But families are great resources for observing human nature in action. Now you'll turn your attention to your own family and explore some of the stories that have been handed down. A family legend doesn't have to be something fancy; it can be any story you've heard repeated. It can be about a family member you know or it can be about one you've never met, perhaps one who lived many years ago.

Begin by Thinking Back over the Many Family Stories You've Heard

You might have heard these stories from family members or from others outside your family. Take time to recall as many as you can think of right now.

Select One You Would Like to Put into Writing

- ✓ Who were the major characters?
- ✓ When and where did it take place?
- ✓ What attracts you most about this story?

Recall the First Time You Ever Heard the Story

Close your eyes and remember hearing it for the first time.

- ✓ How old were you?
- ✓ Where were you?
- ✓ Who told the story?
- ✓ Who else was there?

Trace All the Subsequent Times You Heard the Story

Briefly review all the versions you've heard of this story.

- ✓ Do they differ significantly?
- ✓ Who told each of the versions?
- ✓ What was left out of each version?
- ✓ What was added?

Describe Which Version You Like Best

Out of all the versions, pick the one you like the best or the one you think most authentic. Think about why you like it best.

Now Imagine the Story in Detail Start to Finish

Using the version you like best, see the story unfold start to finish, as if you are watching a movie.

- ✓ Where does the story take place?
- ✓ Who is the central character?
- ✓ What important action happens?
- ✓ What is the climax of the story?
- ✓ How does it end?

Open Your Eyes and Think Back to the Various Tellings of the Family Legend

- ✓ Who told the version you like best?
- ✓ What relationship does the teller of the story have with the main character in the legend?

───────■───────

✍ WRITING WARM-UP

- ✓ Draw a graph of the version you like best, indicating each of the major events in the legend. Label the events clearly, being sure to indicate what you think is the climax of the story.

- ✓ Write a paragraph summarizing the story briefly. Explain when and where you first heard the story and how it affected you.

✍ WRITING ABOUT THE EXPERIENCE

- ✓ Repeated stories exist within families for a reason. Write a journal entry speculating on why you think this story is important in your family. What ideals, hopes, dreams, fears, or despairs does it reveal about your family? What connection can you make between this legend and yourself?

- ✓ Narrate the story as you heard it. Make clear who is the central character and what the climax of the story is. Include in the narrative the story of how, when, and where you heard it for the first time. Compare different versions if you get more than one. End by explaining how you think the story has contributed to the values and heritage of your family.

- ✓ Let the central character in the legend speak and tell the story in his or her own words. Use "I." Get into the character's head and let your imagination guide you into embellishing the story with new details.

✍ EXPANDING THE EXPERIENCE

✓ In a small group, exchange family legends. Compare them as to the historical era in which they occurred, central characters, sequence of events, and the family member who tells the story. After you have had a chance to repeat the family legend orally, write the legend again. This time, however, you will tell the story from another character's point of view—perhaps a very minor one. How does seeing the story through this character's eyes change it?

Family stories such as you have just recalled have supplied many writers with material for their life's work. You can become your family's archivist or storyteller. If possible, take some time now to tape-record interviews with older family members. These interviews will be treasures for both you and future generations and they can become valuable sources for your own writings.

✓ Write about your family from a historical point of view. This is where interviews with older relatives will be invaluable. You can also read genealogical material available from many sources, family papers, and books that detail the history which your family was part of.

- What specific ethnic group does you family belong to?
- What contributions has this ethnic group made to society?
- What is the history of your particular family?
- What part have they played in history?

Write a general account which introduces the ethnic group to others and end your paper by explaining why and how you and your family fit into this group.

✓ Take one aspect of your family history—for example, a grandfather who helped build the first skyscrapers, an aunt who was a nurse during the Crimean War—and place it into the larger historical picture. If your grandfather helped to build skyscrapers in Chicago, find out about the building of skyscrapers during his lifetime. Write a paper placing your relative in the context of history. Include personal interviews about the topic with other relatives if possible.

Exercise 4
People
THE OTHER

The Other. What comes to mind when you see those words? An alien creature? A disgusting person? Someone totally unlike yourself? Or perhaps some shadowy figure that frightens you? Seeing ourselves as not–the other is essential for experiencing our individuality. But carried too far, feeling separate from others can be a lonely and embittering experience. In this exercise you will have an opportunity to explore yourself in relationship to others.

Take Time to Relax Mentally and Physically

Spend a few moments taking deep, spiraling breaths and feel yourself turning inward. Let all your thoughts go and feel an expansion of both mental and physical space. Stay with it until you get a real sense of yourself.

Imagine Yourself Alone

Get a picture of yourself in a situation where you are totally alone—perhaps in your room listening to music, on a park bench looking at the trees, driving a car with only your thoughts to keep you company. Go through several instances when you are usually alone.

✓ How do you usually feel when alone?
✓ What do you usually think about when you're alone?

Now Imagine that Other People Are with You

Run through times when you are normally with other people. See yourself in a variety of situations, with a number of different people. Notice any similarities and differences in how you feel.

Reflect on How You Usually Are with Others

Think about how you feel and act when you are with

✓ one other person you know well;
✓ a group of other people you know well;
✓ one other person you don't know well;
✓ a group of other people you don't know well.

Imagine Yourself in a Group of Strangers

Visualize yourself in a crowd of strangers, people who look and act different from you.

✓ What are your major feelings?
✓ What are your strongest thoughts?
✓ What do you want?

People 111

Now See Yourself Face-to-Face with a Person You Fear or Dislike

Imagine that one person out of the crowd of strangers comes up to you, looks you in the eye, and says something to you.

- ✓ Who is the person?
- ✓ What does the person say?
- ✓ How do you feel?

Open Your Eyes and Think About the Kind of Person You Visualized

Was this a surprise to you in any way?

✍ WRITING WARM-UP

- ✓ In a paragraph, describe "the other" you imagined.
- ✓ Take the sentences you wrote and arrange them into the form of a poem. Add any other sentences you feel are necessary to complete the piece, and then give it an appropriate title.

✍ WRITING ABOUT THE EXPERIENCE

- ✓ Write an account of what you experienced during the exercise. Were you aware of yourself and your feelings throughout? Did you discover anything about yourself in relation to others?
- ✓ Describe a time when you felt connected to a person you had previously felt was a stranger or even your enemy.

✍ EXPANDING THE EXPERIENCE

As the globe shrinks, we hear more and more about how we are all one, how imperative it is that we give up thinking "us and them." Yet we are all still divided into genders, races, and classes: There are those who beg for our money on the streets and those who live in mansions we never enter; there are those with skin lighter than ours and those with skin darker; there are those who speak a language we can't understand and those who speak words we refuse to hear.

- ✓ Choose a particular race, class, or ethnic group you feel prejudiced against. Write a preliminary paper in which you express all your feelings and attitudes about these people. Then gather a few articles or books and read with an open mind about this race or group:

- Where did they originate?
- How did they get where they are now?
- What do they want?
- What do they have and know that others might benefit from?

Learn about the hardships they have been through and include this also in your paper.

With the rise of psychology, the theory of projection—projecting our own unacceptable, buried feelings and ideas onto others—has become better known. Projections are neither bad nor good. If we become aware of them they can lead us into accepting ourselves—and others. A first step in becoming aware of our own projections is in embracing the dark parts of ourselves, the shadow side as described by the American poet Robert Bly:

> We notice that when sunlight hits the body, the body turns bright, but it throws a shadow, which is dark. The brighter the light, the darker the shadow. Each of us has some part of our personality that is hidden from us. Parents, and teachers in general, urge us to develop the light side of the personality—move into well-lit subjects such as mathematics and geometry—and to become successful. The dark part then becomes starved.

—Robert Bly
A Little Book on the Human Shadow

✓ To understand more about projections and your own dark side, read Bly's 81-page book from which the above quotation comes. Or you might want to read Joseph Conrad's story "The Secret Sharer," the definitive dramatization of the shadow figure inside all of us. After you've sparked your own ideas with some reading, write a paper in which you objectively set forth what you have learned about shadow sides—both your own and others. Include any information you've gained about projections, their dangers, and uses.

People 113

Chapter 11

——— PLACES ———

Houses, roads, avenues are as fugitive, alas, as the years.

—Marcel Proust
Swann's Way

Ringed around all our memories, moments, and experiences are the places where these events occur. Whenever something has happened to us, it has happened to us *somewhere*. In the exercises that follow, you will have opportunities to revisit some of those places, both real and imaginary, where you acted out moments of your life.

- *A Place You Know*
- *A Place That Used to Be*
- *A Place You've Never Been*
- *Home*

Exercise 1
Places
A PLACE YOU KNOW

Grandma's house, a beaver dam, a favorite restaurant, a locker room, your bedroom—particular places like these are sometimes filled with significance. Often a place can become as alive as a human being.

Take Yourself to a Place You Know Well

Close your eyes and imagine yourself traveling safely through dark space. Suddenly you land in the middle of a place you know well, a place with which you have had much experience.

Walk Slowly Throughout the Place

If the place is a house or building, go through all the rooms and notice what's in each of them. If the place is an exterior landscape, walk through every area of it, looking at each thing you pass.

✓ What are the most distinguishing characteristics of it?
✓ What do you like most about it?

Observe Every Different Part of It

Look for the normal, expected elements of the place as well as anything that distinguishes it. Do you see anything you've never noticed before? If so, take time to see it vividly.

Open Up All Your Senses

Use all five of your senses to take in the place completely. Notice closely

✓ the different shapes;
✓ the colors;
✓ the textures;
✓ the sounds and smells associated with it.

Visualize a Brief History of Yourself with the Place

With your eyes still closed, run through your life with this place. Start with your first memory of it and take yourself through each stage, ending with the present.

Remember Yourself in One Vivid Moment in the Place

Bring to mind one moment which stands out in your memory which you associate with the place:

✓ Who is with you?
✓ What are you doing?
✓ What is your relationship to the place at this moment?
✓ Why is this memory significant for you?

Return to the Present and Open Your Eyes

Reflect on your relationship to this place.

✓ How do you usually feel when you are there?
✓ What makes it special to you?
✓ What part does it play now in your life?

———————————■———————————

✍ WRITING WARM-UP

✓ Draw a layout of your place. Indicate with an "X" and a word or two the most important spots.

✓ In a single paragraph, briefly describe your place and say what it has meant to you over the years.

✍ WRITING ABOUT THE EXPERIENCE

✓ Write a brief history of how and when this place has been part of your life. Develop your historical account chronologically, expanding with more details and descriptions the most important moment which took place there. End by explaining your feelings about the place and why it is special to you.

✓ You can also write an essay about your place which focuses on the inner events which have happened to you there. How has the place affected the way you have grown up? What attitudes and insights have you gained from it? If you write your essay from this internal point of view, you should still include some external descriptions of your place so your reader can see it vividly.

✍ EXPANDING THE EXPERIENCE

Here are two short descriptions which give specific spatial details. One is from a short story and written in past tense; the other from a book of nonfiction with photographs, written in present tense.

It was a nice house, inside and outside both. In the first place, it had three rooms. The front room was papered in holly paper, with green palmettos from the swamp spaced at careful intervals over the walls. There was fresh newspaper cut with fancy borders on the mantel-shelf, on which were propped photographs of old or very young men printed in faint yellow—Solomon's people. Solomon had a houseful of furniture. There was a double settee, a tall scrolled rocker and an organ in the front room, all around a three-legged table with a pink marble top, on which was set a lamp with three gold feet, besides a jelly glass with pretty hen feathers in it. . . .

—Eudora Welty
"Livvie"

The smokehouse is about eight feet square and about seven tall to the peak of the roof. It is built of vertical boards of uniform width. The door is flush to the wall without a frame and is held shut by a wood button. On the uphill side, at center of the wall and flat to it, hangs a nearly new washtub, the concentrics on its bottom circle like a target. Its galvanized material is brilliant and dryly eating in the sun; the wood of the wall itself is not much less brilliant. The natural usage of a smokehouse is to smoke and store meat, but meat is not smoked here: this is a storage house. . . .

—James Agee (with Walker Evans, photographer)
Let Us Now Praise Famous Men

✓ Study one of the above paragraphs to give you ideas for spatial description. Then write a detailed, step-by-step description of your place, as if you were giving someone a leisurely tour. Take your time. Go through every single spot, describing it with such specific and concrete details that another person can actually see it. End your essay by explaining some major significance of the place—what it means to you, why a place like this is important to others, what vital function such a place serves in the world, and so forth.

Exercise 2
Places **A PLACE THAT USED TO BE**

Places come and places go. Sometimes they quietly disappear. One day you turn around and suddenly they're gone. The gas station on the corner gets boarded up overnight. A tornado rips through a small town and blows the movie theater away in minutes. The drive-in restaurant you used to love becomes a one-hour photo shop or the field you used to play ball in becomes a parking lot. Houses get torn down, dead ends become throughway streets, mansions become museums. You get the picture. In this exercise you'll recall some of those places you used to know that are no more.

Close Your Eyes and Think About Places You Used to Go

Take a few minutes to breathe, close your eyes, and run back through your memory. Think of places where some important—and even some not-so-important—moments of your life took place. Run briefly through several places.

Think About What Has Happened to Some of Those Places

✓ Which of those places have changed into something else?
✓ Which of those places have totally disappeared?

Choose One of the Places to Work With

Take yourself back in time to the place as it used to be:

- ✓ What is it?
- ✓ Where is it located?
- ✓ What is most important about the place?

Take a Full Tour Throughout the Place

With your eyes still closed, walk slowly throughout the place and note everything you observe:

- ✓ What are the dimensions of the place?
- ✓ How does it look on the outside?
- ✓ On the inside?
- ✓ What are the specific shapes, colors, and materials which compose this place?

Look Closely at the Most Distinguished Feature

Now examine in detail the most distinguishing feature of the place. What stands out most for you? Look at it closely, noting all the unusual qualities which appeal most to you. How would you describe the most special quality of the place?

Remember Yourself in Relationship to the Place

Think about your history with this place.

- ✓ How often did you go there?
- ✓ What did you do there most of the time?
- ✓ Why was it important to you?

Recollect a Single Memory of Being in the Place

Now zero in on one particular moment which stands out in all of your memories of being there:

- ✓ What are you doing?
- ✓ Who is with you?
- ✓ What part does the place play in the scene?
- ✓ Why does this particular moment stand out for you?

Open Your Eyes and Bring Yourself into the Present

Allow the scene to dissolve and open your eyes. Sit quietly and reflect on what you experienced. Briefly remember the chronological history of the place—what it used to be like, how it changed, what happened to it.

———■———

WRITING WARM-UP

✓ Make a list, in chronological order, of all the changes the place has been through. Put dates and descriptions by each if you are able to do so.

✓ In one paragraph, describe the significance of this place for you. Include how you feel about it now in retrospect, especially if it no longer exists in the same form.

WRITING ABOUT THE EXPERIENCE

✓ Write a journal entry about the most important moment you spent in the place. Be sure to include how the place contributed to the experience.

✓ Write a chronological history of the place—all you can remember about it. If it went through numerous changes (both physical and functional), give all the details you're able to about each change. Include your own experiences in the place, expanding with specific details the moment you felt was most important. End your essay by stating why the place was significant for you.

✓ Using this place as a general symbol, write an essay in which you illustrate how its individual history is part of a larger history. In other words, you will use the specific place to illustrate a general statement about how places change—and what those changes mean to us as a society.

EXPANDING THE EXPERIENCE

Places and buildings change and disappear under the wheels of our progressing civilization. The great plantations and sweeping ranches are no longer central images in our sense of place. Once there were few buildings and vast land; now we have vast buildings and little land.

✓ With several friends or classmates, discuss the ways our increasing civilization has changed the landscape we live in. Start with your own personal experiences and then broaden the discussion so that you include other geographical areas which you know something about. Keep talking until you find some idea you feel strongly about—such as the need for environmental protection of open land, the need for city ordinances against high-rise buildings, or the importance of zoning laws for new buildings and businesses. Do some wide reading about this idea—read about it from several different angles. Interview people. Come up with information to back up your opinion. Then write a paper in which you present your point of view and argue for it strongly as an idea which must be addressed. End your paper by offering specific solutions to the problem.

✓ With your group (or alone), brainstorm about all the famous places in history which no longer exist in the original form. These can be buildings, towns, sites of important events, and so forth. Choose one that interests you most. Find out all you can about one of these and then write a paper in which you describe the place as it used to be, give its history, and explain in further detail the most important event (or events) which happened there. End by explaining how it disappeared, if you're able to find specific information about this. Include illustrations or photographs when possible.

Exercise 3
Places
A PLACE YOU'VE NEVER BEEN

We have all yearned to visit places we've either heard about or read about. Even if we never get there, the places that we imagine can still be rich sources of pleasure and inspiration for us. In this exercise you will recall a place you've often imagined but have never been to.

Think of Some Places You Have Imagined

These places should be actual physical places such as a building, a city, a country, someone else's house, a college, or any place you've heard or read about but have never visited. Make a quick mental list.

Choose One Place and Visualize It

Close your eyes and see what pictures come into your mind as you think of this place. Pay attention to words and feelings which pop into your mind as you visualize this place you've never been.

Take a Walking Tour

Now take yourself on a tour of the place. Walk slowly through each area, noticing every physical characteristic. Don't stop to wonder whether you're being "right" or not.

✓ How far away is this space from where you are now?
✓ What are the major parts or sections of the place?
✓ Do you see anything that surprises you?
✓ Which part attracts your attention most?

Spend Time in One Particular Spot

Choose one area that attracts you most and put yourself into it.

✓ What do you see yourself doing?
✓ How do you feel in this place?
✓ How close does it come to your fantasies about it?

Take Your Leave

As you complete your tour and prepare to leave, pay attention to what major aspect of the place you take with you. What is most important about it to you?

Return to the Present and Open Your Eyes

With your eyes open, run through the entire scene again:

✓ What were your major images?
✓ What was the most outstanding characteristic of this place?

✍ WRITING WARM-UP

✓ Write down one word which best describes your feelings about this place. Then write one paragraph which will expand the meaning of that word.

✓ Draw one simple sketch which interprets your experience. This can be a realistic drawing or just an abstract figure which symbolizes the place to you. Afterward, add one or two written sentences which will explain the significance of your drawing.

✍ WRITING ABOUT THE EXPERIENCE

✓ Write a physical description of the place as you imagined it, moving from one space to the other and describing each spot in detail. If you get stuck for details, briefly close your eyes and return to the experience of the exercise. Write down what you actually *saw*, no matter how imaginary. If it seems important, you can also contrast the imaginary experience you just had with how you have previously thought about the place. Did you discover any new details about the place from your imaginary tour? If possible, find out if they were accurate.

✓ Write a memory piece about a place you often imagined as a child and later went to, such as a relative's house, the circus, a carnival, the beach, or a nearby town. Compare the place you imagined from the things you heard about it with how the place actually appeared to you when you actually saw it. Explain whether you were fulfilled or disappointed. Keep the childhood perspective as much as possible throughout your paper so that you capture a child's point of view of the place.

✍ EXPANDING THE EXPERIENCE

✓ An old song, "Far Away Places," sums up this feeling of longing for imagined places in about 16 lines. If possible, get the sheet music for this song and study the words—or listen to one of the recent recordings of it by Willie Nelson and Leon Russell. Then write an essay about why you think people long for places they've never been to. What is the meaning of this common human feeling? Use your own experience as a central example.

✓ Choose one place you've always felt drawn to but one which you've never visited. It can be the one you used in the exercise or another one. It can be a place across the seas or one nearby, but make it specific. Instead of a country, choose a city or a village in that country; you can even pick one particular spot in one city. (You might also be interested in places where famous events have taken place.) Locate reading materials, photos, or films about the place and study it until you get to know it thoroughly. Imagine that you are going to visit there one day. What would you need to know ahead of time? In your paper, tell all you have found out about the place, concentrating on the aspect most intriguing to you. Include any new feelings and perceptions you now have about the place after reading more about it.

✓ But perhaps the place you long to see is an imaginary one. Maybe you've always dreamed of visiting Oz or The Shire or Erewhon. If reading has supplied you with fantasies of imaginary places, here's a book made just for you: The Dictionary of Imaginary Places by Alberto Manguel and Gianni Guadalupi, a 400-page book filled with illustrations, maps, and detailed descriptions of hundreds of imaginary places created by writers. You'll find information on places such as Utopia, Shangri-La, Emerald City, and many pages on specific writers such as Ursula K. Le Guin, J. R. R. Tolkien, Edgar Rice Burroughs, Frank Baum, and C. S. Lewis. If you can locate this book, use it as a starting point for your research. Choose one writer who has created an imaginary place. (If the writer has created more than one place, choose only one of the places.) Read several works by the writer that take place in this imaginary place. Then write a paper in which you describe the place, the people, and the activities there, using examples from the literature to illustrate your points.

HOME

Home—the zenith of all places. But more than just a place, home is also a powerful concept. Our language is full of the importance of home: "a home away from home"; "keep the home fires burning"; "there's no place like home"; "home is where the heart is"; "this feels like home"; "make yourself at home." Some people are fortunate to feel at home any place. Others never find a home even if they own houses. Obviously, home is both a place and something beyond a place. This exercise will lead you through some of the ideas and feelings you have about home.

Make a Short List of Other Expressions That Use Home

Expand on the list given above. Think about the literal use of home—"to go home"—and the symbolic use of the word—"Anywhere I hang my hat is home."

Explore Your Own Ideas of Home

Now quickly make a list of all the words and feelings you personally associate with the idea of home.

Close Your Eyes and Remember Times You Felt at Home

Focus your attention on a spot on the floor and sit quietly remembering the major times in your life when you've had a feeling of home. Just keep them in your mind as you enter deeper into the exercise.

Travel Back to the Very First Home You Remember as a Child

Close your eyes and go backward in time to the very first home you remember as a child. Visualize every aspect of it. If this home is the same home you still live in, visualize how it was then as compared to now. See yourself in it as a young child.

✓ What was your home like on the outside?
✓ Visualize every aspect of the interior. Move through every room.
✓ What part of it was most important to you?
✓ Where did you sleep? Where did you play? Where did you eat?

Remember All the Other Homes You've Lived In

Bring yourself up through the years to the present time and briefly visualize each of the other homes you've lived in until now. If you've lived in the same home all your life, remember all the stages of its development, and how it has changed over the years.

✓ What did these homes have in common?
✓ How were they different from each other?
✓ Which one did you like most and why?

Visualize the Place You Now Live In

Take time to go slowly through the place that is now your home. If it is the same home you have lived in all your life, contrast how it used to be with how it is now.

✓ How do you feel about the place you live in now?
✓ What is special about it?
✓ How is it different from other homes you've lived in?
✓ How do you feel in this home?

Create a Place in Your Mind That Is Your Perfect Home

If you are not now living in your perfect home, imagine exactly how your ideal home would be. Visualize how it would look on the outside and what it would consist of on the inside.

✓ What aspect of this home would be most special to you?
✓ What do you see yourself doing in your ideal home?
✓ How would you feel there that would be different from how you feel now?

✎ WRITING WARM-UP

✓ Make a list of all the homes you've ever lived in.

✓ Write two paragraphs which explain what the word "home" means to you. Include any new realizations which came to you during the exercise.

✍ WRITING ABOUT THE EXPERIENCE

✓ Draw a floor plan of the room you slept in as a child. Label each part. Notice where you feel the most emotion as you study the room. Now write a short essay about your room as a child and what it meant to you.

✓ Describe the most favorite home you've ever lived in. You can include a drawing of the floor plan if you like. After you describe it physically, explain which parts of it meant the most to you and why. What about it made you feel at home? When and where do you have that same feeling today?

✍ EXPANDING THE EXPERIENCE

Not too many years ago, people were born in one house, lived their lives in it, and then died there. Now we live in a world where people are on the go, often uprooting themselves several times, and living in a series of different kinds of homes.

Because the feelings about home are so intense, films and literature often use this idea as a central metaphor. One of the fullest treatments of this idea of home is E. M. Forster's *Howards End*. In the passage that follows, Mrs. Wilcox, who has lived in Howards End all her life, expresses sympathy for Margaret Schlegel, a young woman who is about to lose the house she has grown up in:

> It is monstrous, Miss Schlegel; it isn't right. I had no idea that this was hanging over you. I do pity you from the bottom of my heart. To be parted from your house, you father's house—it oughtn't be allowed. It is worse than dying. I would rather die than—Oh, poor girls! Can what they call civilization be right, if people mayn't die in the room where they were born?

> —E. M. Forster
> *Howards End*

✓ Write a paper in which you respond to the above idea. What are your thoughts about people moving around and changing homes? If possible, read the book *Howards End* or see the movie. Or read other pieces in which this concept of one home for life is discussed. Include in your paper any observations and insights you gain from other sources.

✓ Contrast our society's idea of what a home is with those of another society—think about various types of dwellings that are used as homes—consider, for example, the Alaskan igloo or the Native American teepee. Choose a type of dwelling that interests you, study illustrated books, and do further reading about it. Then write an illustrated paper in which you describe this home, contrasting it with the houses

126 *Places / Home*

most of us live in. Include the significance of this home to the people who live in it.

✓ Most of us live in single-family dwellings, either alone or with family or friends. Expand your concept of living styles and do some reading about people who live in groups. Communal living, in which people share both work and responsibilities but thereby gain other freedoms, is not as popular in this country as it was in the 1960s and 1970s; but the idea continues to be a universal one that a large variety of people embrace. Right now there are many long-established groups who live and work together in this country—and they are not all considered "cults."

Conduct a study of communal living in this country, assessing both the benefits and the drawbacks, the successes and the failures. You can focus on one current successful group which interests you and write a paper that traces the development and growth of the communal-living group, indicating what their status is today. Or you can focus on one of the early communal-living groups in this country, such as Brook Farm in the mid-1800s, and trace its history. Or, expand your research and write your paper on the history of commune living in America. Either way, assess the benefits and the drawbacks and explain the successes and failures of communal living.

Chapter 12

———— EVENTS ————

The performance is always the same;
it is only the actors who change.

—Marcus Aurelius
Meditations

Things happen. And sometimes these things repeat themselves with alarming regularity. All of us at one time or another have been mesmerized by events happening to others a continent away and feeling all the while as if we were center-stage actors in the drama. As the globe shrinks, most events, both great and small, have enormous repercussions that affect us in some way—even those of us who are distant from the event itself and untouched by the reality of it. The exercises in this section give you a way to look at yourself in relationship to important events in the world.

- *Today's News*
- *A Blood-Boiling Issue*
- *A Modern Hero*
- *A Moment in History*

Exercise 1
Events
TODAY'S NEWS

You don't have to look far to get hooked into the world of outer events. Today's news will serve perfectly. Every day we are bombarded with news; some of it we want to hear and some of it we don't. For this exercise, you are consciously going to select the *one* piece of today's news that means something to you.

Before Beginning the Exercise, Think of Yourself and the News

Take a few minutes to assess what kind of news receptor you are. What's your style?

✓ Do you gobble up all the news?
✓ Avoid it?
✓ Take it running throughout the day?
✓ Spend concentrated time with it?

Make a Brief List of All the Ways You Receive the News

Quickly make a list of how you get the news throughout the day. Put an asterisk by your favorite ways.

Now Close Your Eyes and Visualize Yourself Going Through Your Day

Close your eyes, take a few deep breaths, and see yourself beginning your day in the usual way. Begin with getting out of bed and then going through your usual routine.

✓ What is the first thing you usually do?
✓ At what point in your day do you receive the day's news?
✓ How does receiving the news usually make you feel?

Zero in on Today's News

Now shift to today's—or yesterday's—news. Go through every aspect of it that you remember hearing or reading about. Take enough time to get down every single piece of news you can remember.

✓ What was the most outstanding piece of news you received?
✓ What news did you like the most? The least?
✓ How did hearing the news make you feel today or yesterday?

Pick One Piece of Today's News to Focus On

Now, with your eyes still closed, focus on the one piece of news that had the most meaning for you. Visually imagine it happening like a movie on your mental screen. If you heard more than one version of it, choose the one you feel is best.

✓ Who is involved?
✓ What is happening?
✓ Where is it happening?
✓ What is at stake?
✓ What is the outcome so far?

Open Your Eyes and Reflect on What You Just Experienced

Take a deep breath, open your eyes, and relax. Even if the news is traumatic to you, bring yourself into the present and begin to think clearly about it. Ask yourself these questions:

✓ Why is this news important to me?
✓ What do I personally want to happen?
✓ What do I think will happen?
✓ What part can I play in this—if any?

✍ WRITING WARM-UP

✓ Take a few minutes to come back completely into the present and see how you feel after reliving this piece of news. Then write down a sentence which expresses your primary feeling about this news.

✓ Write a paragraph in which you give your opinions, your hopes, or your recommendations about this event.

✍ WRITING ABOUT THE EXPERIENCE

✓ In your journal, write a brief analysis of yourself as a receptor of the news. How do you generally respond to the news? How objective are you? How broad a coverage do you need to feel satisfied?

✓ Describe in detail the piece of today's news that you visualized during the exercise. If you got information from more than one source, indicate which information you got from each source. Give your opinion of each of your sources of information.

✍ EXPANDING THE EXPERIENCE

✓ With a small group of friends or classmates, conduct a discussion of the current news. Keep it current—within the last two weeks. Together compile a list of all the news items each of you has heard about. Let everyone give the information he or she has found. Keep talking until you bring the event up to date. As the discussion proceeds, listen for contradicting information. Find out where specific information has come from. After the discussion, study several news sources, such as different newspapers, national and local television news and radio stations, and news magazines such as *Newsweek*, *Time*, and *U.S. News and World Report*. Compare how two or three of these sources have reported the same news event. Write a paper highlighting the differences in the news sources, giving specific examples from the reports themselves as illustration. Conclude your paper by telling what you have learned through this discussion and study about how the news is reported. Attach pertinent clippings to the end of your paper if appropriate.

✓ Choose one news event which currently interests you. Follow the reporting of this event for a period of two weeks. Keep a record of when and where you get new information. What changes occur in the event itself? What changes occur in the reporting? Write an analysis of news coverage which uses the event as the central example. Explain, from your point of view, the pattern which most news coverage follows and end your paper with an evaluation. Do you think most of the news coverage is accurate? Predictable? Subject to change? Unbiased? Come up with your own opinions.

Exercise 2
Events

A BLOOD-BOILING ISSUE

Much goes on in this world that is inhumane, as well as insane. Every day we are confronted with a "real" world in which lies, murders, and injustices seem to be common fare. Some of these surreal events may have touched your own life in different ways. Here is an exercise that will give you the chance to take some current issue which makes your blood boil and have your full say about it.

Think About This World You Now Live In

Take a few minutes to reflect on the current state of the world as you know it. Yes, there are good things. But in this exercise you want to focus on the things that are not-so-good—that are, in fact, blood-boiling to you.

Make a List of All the Things That Upset You About This World

Without stopping to analyze whether you're being fair or rational, quickly make a list of events and issues that upset you in any way. For this exercise, forget personal problems and concentrate on problems in the society around you or in the world at large.

Choose One Issue to Work With

From your list, choose one particular issue to work with. Be sure it is one that bothers you enough to get your temper up. Close your eyes and take a few

132   *Events / A Blood-Boiling Issue*

deep breaths so your mind relaxes. Now think about the many different aspects of this issue.

✓ What is the most important aspect of this issue for you?
✓ What part about it makes you most angry?

Visualize Different Incidents in Which This Issue Has Manifested Itself

Run through as many incidents as you can remember. These should include real (not fictionalized) incidents you've both seen and found out about from other sources, such as television, radio, newspapers and magazines, and other people. Take time to recreate the images that you imagined and also saw in real photographs.

Focus on One Specific Incident That Symbolizes the Issue for You

Choose one event that you feel sums up the issue most dramatically. With your eyes still closed, run through it slowly and recapture all you know about it.

✓ Who are the people involved?
✓ Where does it take place?
✓ What is at stake?
✓ What is the outcome?
✓ How is this different from what you want to happen?

Now Open Your Eyes and Think About What You've Experienced

Mentally run back through the major incident and check in with your own feelings.

✓ What is your most intense response to this event?
✓ Why does this event epitomize the issue for you?

Think About Some Solutions or Ideas for Solving This Issue

✓ What are some things that could be done to change things?
✓ What actions could you personally imagine taking?

———————■———————

✍ WRITING WARM-UP

✓ Study the list you made at the beginning of the exercise. Add to it any new ones you discovered. Look over your list and draw lines to any of them that seem connected. Work on your list long enough to organize most of your concerns into two to four groups and then give each group a unifying title.

✓ In a short poem or a paragraph, commemorate the specific incident you visualized above. Allow your feelings about the issue to shape your words.

✍ WRITING ABOUT THE EXPERIENCE

✓ Write a journal entry in which you let fly all your frustration and anger over this blood-boiling issue. Say everything you've been wanting to say about it. Later you can go back and write an essay which is more logical and coherent, but first express all your opinions and feelings in whatever way they come up.

✓ Now bring the issue even closer to home: Write a paper exploring all the ways this issue affects your own life. First present the issue, making it sound important and life-affecting; then logically classify every effect you feel it has on your life. End by giving thought to what you, personally, can do about this issue.

✍ EXPANDING THE EXPERIENCE

✓ After you've looked at the issue from several personal angles, step back and look at it more objectively: how it affects others, how it shapes the world we live in, and so forth. Now is the time to do some general reading about the issue. Look at it historically as well as currently. Form a strong opinion. Then write a paper in which you argue in favor of your position about the issue, explaining the problems the issue causes. End your paper by suggesting one or two strong solutions to these problems.

The United States of America was created out of protest, and protest continues to be a major vehicle for shaping the destiny of this country. Nearly all protest begins with individual response to issues of the day—personal response such as you have created through doing this exercise.

✓ Form a small group for discussion. You will probably need several sessions for this subject. Begin by having all the members of the group contribute the three major issues which concern them. Decide on a time limit for each issue and then discuss the issue for that length of time. Keep working until the group comes up with a single issue that all the members agree is blood-boiling. At some point, have each member freewrite about the issue. Before the next session, each member should do some reading and, if possible, interview a key person in an organization that is protesting the issue—organizations working in such areas as abortion (pro-life or pro-choice), government waste, drunk driving, pollution, drug control, and so forth. There are usually local chapters that can be found through the telephone yellow pages. An excellent source for getting a current overview of important issues (for example, boycotts, the draft, youth gangs, world hunger, and water supply) is *The CQ Researcher* which is published weekly. Each issue is devoted to one topic and offers an annotated bibliography that will lead you to additional sources. After the group has gathered together enough information, present your findings orally to the rest of the class. If a group project is not possible, you can do this individually and write up your findings in an essay.

✓ Another direction you might go with this is to follow the movement historically. When did it first begin? Who started it? How has it changed over the course of time? What has it accomplished? What is the current situation? Note: You might also be interested in a movement that accomplished what it set out to do and is no longer an issue, such as the women's suffrage movement, the organization of labor into unions, or early prison reforms.

Exercise 3
Events
A MODERN HERO

The word "hero" is a loaded term and one that can cover a lot of territory. We have cultural heroes, personal heroes, political heroes, heroes of the moment, even fallen heroes. For this exercise, think of the word hero as being any person—male or female—you think has set a high standard for others to follow. Your hero may or may not have risked personal danger or triumphed over evil; but she or he may have, in some quiet way, done something you think is deserving of the word hero.

Reflect on Your Own Ideas of the Meaning of Hero

What does that word mean to you? What images does it conjure up? Jot down a few words which you associate with the term.

Make a List of Modern Heroes You Admire

Make a list of modern-day women and men whom you most admire. The list can include people living or dead, famous or not widely known, so long as they are fairly contemporary figures. You might also want to include on your list people you know personally who are not necessarily famous.

Think About What Makes These People Heroes

Beside each person's name, list the quality and or actions you find most outstanding.

Choose One Person to Work with Further

From your list, choose one person to work with. Close your eyes and call up a mental image of the person. Recollect all the things you can remember about this person. Think about his or her

- ✓ physical appearance
- ✓ background and upbringing
- ✓ life's circumstances
- ✓ outstanding characteristics

Let Your Hero's Life Play Before Your Eyes

With your eyes still closed, recollect all the circumstances of your hero's life. Fill in as many details as possible from what you've read or heard.

- ✓ What is the primary focus of your hero's life?
- ✓ In what ways is this primary focus demonstrated?

Imagine Your Hero in Action

With your eyes still closed, imagine your hero taking action. These actions can be your own creation or things you've actually read about or seen.

- ✓ What do you remember most?
- ✓ What do you see that you consider important actions?
- ✓ What motivates your hero to take these actions?

Open Your Eyes and Think About What You Saw

Let the scene dissolve, open your eyes and think about what you just experienced.

- ✓ What still stands out in your mind?
- ✓ What differences are there in what actually happened and what you imagined?
- ✓ What, if anything, would you like to change about what you saw?

Reflect on Why This Hero Is a Hero to You

Take a few more moments to consider why this person is a hero to you.

✓ What emotions does she or he inspire in you?
✓ Which of this hero's qualities would you like to have for yourself?

✍ WRITING WARM-UP

✓ Write down the name of your hero and how you feel about her or him. Then write a sentence explaining the quality you most admire and would like to acquire for yourself.

✓ In your journal, write down your ideas about what it means to be a hero. Avoid just the general stereotypes of brave actions, fearlessness, courage, and so forth. Get to the very bottom of what *you* consider heroic.

✍ WRITING ABOUT THE EXPERIENCE

✓ Write an essay in which you define the word hero according to your own ideas and then show how your hero fulfills this definition. Be sure to give evidence, through the details of his or her life, to back up what you say.

✓ As a child, you might have had favorite heroes you've now replaced. In what ways is this modern hero like the heroes of your childhood? What particular qualities do they share in common? What might your admiration of these heroes teach you about your own life? Write a paper in which you trace the development of your hunger for heroes starting with your own childhood and coming into the present. End with what you have learned from these heroes and how they have affected your life.

✍ EXPANDING THE EXPERIENCE

Even though sexism in language is a big issue today, most of the current dictionaries continue to define hero as *male*. But hero is a generic term for both women and men. In *The Handbook of Nonsexist Writing*, the authors, Casey Miller and Kate Swift, state:

> The word *hero* applies to males and females alike; the word *heroine*, although it has a long, honorable history going back to the Greek *heroine* (counterpart of the masculine-gender *heros*), is anomalous. Its use today presents the same prob-

lem as any other English word used specifically of a female when no comparable masculine-gender term exists: it makes females nonstandard.

✓ Explore further this problem of gender in heroes. In a small group, allow each member to discuss his or her idea about whether a hero is usually male or female. A good place to start the discussion is to go back and see how many females each of you put on your list of heroes at the beginning of the exercise. Think about how each of you has changed ideas over the years and also how current popular opinion has changed on this issue. After the discussion, write a paper in which you discuss your own concepts of the two words "hero" and "heroine." You can include the impressions you used to have and what you have now found out. Concentrate on the *qualities* you think make up a hero and discuss whether or not those are gender-related.

In his book *The Hero with a Thousand Faces* Joseph Campbell states: "It is not society that is to guide and save the creative hero, but precisely the reverse." He means by this that as a society we must look to the heroes themselves to guide us—and, in fact, we may even create these heroes just so they will do that. Think about the role of heroes in creating a better society:

✓ What ideals do we endow heroes with in order for them to guide us?

✓ How have these ideals changed during the course of history?

✓ After doing some reading and reflection on the purpose of the hero in society, write a paper in which you explain why we must have heroes and how we make use of them in order to create a more ideal world. Point out specific qualities we attribute to the hero and explain how these qualities serve to lead us to higher ideals. You can use heroes from history, fiction, or real life in order to illustrate your points.

Exercise 4
Events
A MOMENT IN HISTORY

Few of us have a direct involvement with major historical events, yet we are all affected by these events in some way, both collectively and individually. Here is an exercise you can use many times to locate yourself during historical moments and then to discover how these moments have affected your life.

Choose One Historical Moment With Which to Work

This should be an event which has taken place during your lifetime. Make certain that this is a historical *moment*—an event which took place in a matter of minutes—for example, the signing of a treaty, a court decision, the assassination of a leader. Naturally there will be many events involved which led up to this moment, but you are concentrating primarily on the very minutes in which the event changed the course of history.

Locate Yourself in Time and Space During This Moment

Once you've selected this historical moment, close your eyes, breathe deeply several times, and then picture yourself traveling back in time. Visualize what the world was like at that time and what was going on in your own life.

✓ How old are you when this moment occurs?
✓ What are your major concerns in life at this time?

Remember When You First Heard About or Witnessed the Event

Relive the moment of hearing or seeing as fully as possible.

✓ Exactly where are you?
✓ What are you doing?
✓ What other people are with you?

Run Through the Events as You Remember Hearing Them

Visualize as vividly as possible the images which came into your imagination as you heard about the event. Some of these images may have come from news photos or television; others may have been created solely by your imagination.

✓ Where does the moment take place?
✓ Who are the main people involved? Who is the most important person?
✓ What exactly happens?
✓ What is the climactic moment?

Examine Your Response in Detail

✓ What is the first thought which runs through your head when you hear the story?

✓ What are your immediate feelings?
✓ What else do you think about?
✓ What action do you take?
✓ What are other people around you doing?

Think About How You Responded Later

Open your eyes and briefly review the scene in your thoughts. Now that you've made yourself part of this moment in history, reflect on what significance this event has for you.

✓ What were your later reactions to this historic moment?
✓ Did it affect your life in any way?

———————■———————

✍ WRITING WARM-UP

✓ Write a journal entry about why this historical event still stands out in your memory.

✓ Write down five to ten separate statements about the event. Then arrange the statements in the form of a poem which will commemorate the event. Play around with the arrangement until you discover some unity among the statements. You might find it necessary to rewrite some of the sentences or to add others.

✍ WRITING ABOUT THE EXPERIENCE

✓ Narrate as vividly as possible where you were and what you were doing at the moment you heard the news. As you write, close your eyes at times to help yourself retrieve more specific details. Was there anything unusual in what happened to you? What are some minute details you noticed then that seem odd to you now? Re-create the time and place in which you heard about this moment as concretely as you can.

✓ Keeping in mind all the facts that you know about the historic moment, write a paper about how the event might have ended differently. How do you wish it had turned out? What were the pivotal moments that could have changed everything?

✍ EXPANDING THE EXPERIENCE

If you haven't done much reading on the historical event, find an article or encyclopedia entry which gives an overview of it. Once you've read a capsule account, see how this fits in with what you already know.

140 *Events / A Moment in History*

✓ How much of your knowledge was accurate? How much inaccurate?
✓ What new information did you discover?

✓ Now spend some time in journal or freewriting to discover a deep conviction you have about this historic moment. Do further research—read books and articles, see movies and documentaries and so forth—and find evidence to support your opinion. Then write a paper giving your convictions about the historic moment. Support your ideas with evidence. If you found evidence contradictory to your own, include it as comparison and argue against it.

✓ With a group of friends or classmates brainstorm about major historical events which you feel have had a big impact on your lives. These should be events which have taken place during your lifetime. After you've come up with a large list, narrow it down and try to agree on the one the group thinks is the most important. Then discuss some of the specific results this historical moment has had—and might still be having—on the present. Either as a group or individual project, do further research on the historic moment and present your findings in an oral report or a paper. Use visuals such as slides and photographs to support your findings. Argue convincingly about the effects this event has had on the course of history.

Part IV

THE WORLD OF INVENTION

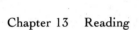

What lies just beyond all that we perceive with our senses? So much richness waits among the cracks of life, between the inner world and the outer. Perhaps there is no name for it, but it is often the place we instinctively return to, the place we feel most alive. This is the world of our own invention, the shadowy domain of dreams, imagination, and mental wanderings. This is the realm beyond, the invisible world which belongs to us in our most intimate moments alone with ourselves.

Chapter 13

———— READING ————

What I sought in books was a world whose surfaces, whose people and events and days lived, actually matched the exaltation of the interior life. There you could live.

—Annie Dillard
An American Childhood

Open a page, enter a world—a world that belongs at once to both you and to someone else. To read is to travel with the mind, the imagination, and the soul faster than the speed of light. In an instant new vistas appear before you, dazzlingly real, potentially transforming. To read is to live a lifetime in a few hours. The exercises in this section will help you remember how active the act of reading can be.

- *Words*
- *A Book Recalled*
- *People on Pages*
- *A Favorite Author Revisited*

Exercise 1
Reading WORDS

One. Two. Three words. What you're reading right now penetrates your brain because something called words is set in front of your eyes. The words follow each other in what you've come to recognize as a logical order. But if we mix it up a bit—what two because words three each—suddenly those same words, still in their same form, become meaningless. What is this magic thing, a word?

Close Your Eyes and Allow Some Words to Pop into Your Mind

Close your eyes, take a few deep breaths, and see which word—or words—pop into your mind. Don't work took hard. Just let the words come and go. Spend a few seconds with each of them.

Relax Further and Travel Back in Time

Take another deep breath and let yourself relax even more. Imagine yourself getting younger and younger until you are a little baby who can't yet talk. But you can hear what others are saying and you understand some of the words you hear:

- ✓ Where are you? Who's with you?
- ✓ What do you hear the grown-ups saying?
- ✓ Which words do you understand?
- ✓ Which of them don't you understand?
- ✓ Which words most attract your attention?

Now Imagine Yourself Getting Older

See yourself growing, toddling around. You have many words in your head. You have a few words on your tongue. Visualize yourself walking around with words in your head and beginning to talk.

- ✓ What are the words you know best in your head?
- ✓ What the words you like to say aloud?

Remember Yourself Looking at a Book

Imagine yourself getting a little older, old enough to look at a book. See the words on the page in front of you.

- ✓ What is the book?
- ✓ What pictures do you see?
- ✓ What words do you see?
- ✓ Which of the words do you understand?

Return to the Present and See Which Words Are Still in Your Head

With your eyes still closed, let some of the words you've recalled bounce around in your head.

- ✓ Which ones are most recurring?
- ✓ Which ones do you like the best?

Choose One of the Words to Work With

Choose the word that has the most meaning for you right now and project it onto a screen in front of your eyes. Enlarge it and examine it closely:

✓ What images come up in your mind as you do so?
✓ Does the word change in any way? How?

Visualize Yourself in the Middle of the Word

Imagine yourself sitting or standing smack in the middle of the word. There's the word in big letters and now there's you in the middle of it. Play around with it:

✓ How do you feel about this word?
✓ What ideas does this word bring to your mind?

Let the Scene Dissolve and Return to the Present

Open your eyes and take a few moments to recount some of the words which came to you through the exercise. Say them over silently to yourself for a few moments. Which words are in your head right now?

✍ WRITING WARM-UP

✓ Write down the word that is now most dominant in your mind. Then write a sentence explaining the significance of the word for you.

✓ Make a list of all the words you can remember knowing and liking from your early childhood. (Be sure to include the first word you ever said if you can remember it.)

✍ WRITING ABOUT THE EXPERIENCE

✓ Write a journal entry about one of the words that means the most to you. Explain how you felt about it when you were little and how you feel about it now. Keep writing until you discover the significance of the word for you. Include any important memories associated with the word.

✓ Choose a word that you really like—or one that you don't like. Write an essay which first defines the word. (Use the dictionary and then expand the definition with your own ideas.) After you have defined the word, explain all the associations (memories, ideas, attitudes) that you have about the word. If re-defining or re-evaluating the word changes your feelings about it, explain that change at the end of your essay.

✓ Write a memoir of one of your first experiences with a word—or words. Close your eyes and return to parts of the exercise if you need more material. Begin with your earliest memory of the word and then trace the word through your life from childhood to the present.

✍ EXPANDING THE EXPERIENCE

The word is a highly charged idea going back to the earliest beginnings of civilization. Before there were letters to form words, pictures (hieroglyphics) were drawn to represent words or sounds. The concept of the word has shaped human destiny as we know it: "In the beginning was the Word . . . ." To give someone your word, to swear by your word, is still considered the most profound evidence of truth. Words hurt. Words heal. Powerful stuff, words.

In his book, *Words as Eggs*, Russell Lockhart, writer and therapist, says:

"At the beginning of everything is a word, a word as seed, a word as egg. . . . Words take on life, induce images, excite the imagination, begin to weave textures with one another, and tell whole stories, if we but scratch the surface of the word."

—Russell Lockhart
Words as Eggs

✓ With a few friends or classmates, come up with a list of words that you like or are interested in. From that list, each person will choose one word to research in depth. Once you have your word, go first to a good, recent dictionary. Try *The American Heritage Dictionary of the English Language* (the large one, not the college edition) which has an Indo-European Roots section at back. When you look up the word, make a careful note of every single definition. If a root word is given as reference, turn to the back and see what it means. Next consult *The Oxford English Dictionary*, a multivolume set of extensive word histories, and study the *etymology* (the origins) of the word. Make careful notes of the many different changes in the word. When the group meets again, each person is responsible for reporting on his or her individual word. Afterwards, you can write up your findings on one word. To keep the paper from being merely a dull listing of what you found, freewrite on what the word means to you personally and what it suggests to your imagination. Then include, as part of your paper, your personal responses to the word, and your own mental wanderings which the word inspires.

✓ Scratch the surface of a word: Pick one word and let it take you on a magic carpet ride. Begin with the word. Put it on paper and then follow it. Let it write the paper for you. This is the process of free-association, of automatic writing, and it can do much to free up your imagination. Give it a try and see what happens. You may surprise yourself—or, at the very least, have some fun.

Exercise 2
Reading
A BOOK RECALLED

When you sit down to read a book, you bring to the reading your past, your present, your hopes, dreams, ideas, fantasies, and everything else that makes up who you are. That is why the way you read a book and what you remember most about it will always be different from anyone else's way. In this exercise you're going to recall a book you read several years ago—and you're going to do it swiftly. You might be surprised at how much you remember both about the book and about your reading of it.

Choose a Book You Read Once Several Years Ago

Think of a book you read a few years back. Any book will do—it doesn't have to be a long one or a classic. It can be a novel, a biography, or any other nonfiction book. The only constraint is *do not pick one you've seen in movie adaptation*. You want all the images you remember to have been created solely by your own mind. (If you choose a book you've read several times, pick one reading of it to work with.)

Recall What It Looked Like in Your Imagination

Close your eyes and visualize the book. Examine it in detail. The physical aspects of the book are important:

- ✓ Was it a paperback or hardcover?
- ✓ What kind of illustration was used on the cover or dustjacket? Were there illustrations elsewhere in the book?
- ✓ What kind of shape was the book in? Was it new or one used by others, such as a library book or a hand-me-down?
- ✓ Were there notes or other markings anywhere on it? Did you write or underline in it?

Run Through the Story Exactly as You Remember It

Keep your eyes closed and try to remember the progression of the narrative. This is not a quiz on the book. Your memory of the story does not have to be faithful to the book. This is about *the* story *you* got from reading the book. If your book is a novel or one with a story line, run through the plot. If you've chosen a book without a story, run through the sequence of ideas or events as they were presented.

Focus in More Detail on the Part You Remember Most

Look more closely at the scene or part that is still most vivid to you.

- ✓ What images do you remember?
- ✓ What people are involved?
- ✓ What words or ideas do you remember?

Put Yourself in Relation to the Book

Think about the book in terms of yourself. What did you bring to the reading of the book?

- ✓ When did the reading take place?
- ✓ Where were you?
- ✓ What was going on in your life at this time?
- ✓ What part of the book moved you most?
- ✓ What was the major idea you got out of the book?

Open Your Eyes and Mentally Go Back Over What You Remembered

Get the story or the sequence of events you've recalled firmly in your mind. At this point you might be agonizing over all you've forgotten. Put that aside and concentrate just on what you remember.

———■———

✍ WRITING WARM-UP

- ✓ Write down the title of the book, the author, and a few sentences that tell what the book is about.

- ✓ Briefly describe the scene or idea from the book which stands out most for you.

✍ WRITING ABOUT THE EXPERIENCE

- ✓ Write down the story of your reading of the book. Explain what was happening in your life at that time and why you were reading this particular book. Vividly show where you were at one moment while you were reading the book and what was going on in your head as you read.

✓ Write an essay about the book completely from memory. Don't worry about missing details or how accurate you are. This is your memory of reading the book. In your paper, avoid chronological summary. Begin with what you think is the most important idea or scene from the book and then move later to a more general discussion. Include why you think you still remember this book. What still stands out for you about it? What did you learn from reading it that made a difference to you?

✐ EXPANDING THE EXPERIENCE

✓ Revisit your book. Find a copy and leaf through it. Notice what catches your eye this time. Read all or part of the book again. Afterward, write a paper in which you compare what you remembered with what is actual. Where there any surprises? How is the book different from what you remembered? Highlight any differences in your paper. Include also as part of your paper your memory of reading the book for the first time and compare yourself as a reader then with yourself as a reader now.

✓ Rewrite parts of the book. If it's a novel or biography, you might rewrite the ending or a scene you'd like to have been different. If it's a book of information or ideas, write important information you think was missing or rewrite passages so that they reflect your own ideas. Make clear which parts of the book you're rewriting and why.

✓ Think of a book (not the same one you've already used in this exercise) you have read that has a dramatic effect on the way you view the world. Find that book and look it over again. Locate the specific passages that affected your thinking. Write a paper which explains the impact of this book on your thinking. Break it down into several segments—that is, explain each idea and illustrate, with examples from your life, how that idea affected you.

Exercise 3
Reading
PEOPLE ON PAGES

People on pages, the ones we meet in novels and short stories, can be as real as those we actually know. Sometimes even more real. You'll have a chance through this exercise to renew your acquaintance with some of those people you met on pages in years past—and perhaps see how you both have changed.

Think Back Over Some of the Novels or Short Stories You've Read

Close your eyes and relax with a few deep breaths and just allow your mind to wander over some of the stories or novels you've read. Let scenes and characters drift in and out of your mind for a few minutes.

Let Some of the Characters Come to Life in Your Mind

Keep your mental movie going and allow some of the characters just to come in and out. Watch what they're doing, how they look, what they're saying.

Choose One Character to Work With

Out of all the characters drifting in and out of your mind, choose one to work with. With your eyes still closed, visualize the character.

- ✓ What does he or she look like?
- ✓ What is the most noticeable about your character?

See Your Character in Action

Visualize your character in action. The action can be a scene from the book or short story or it can be something you are making up. Observe your character's

- ✓ appearance
- ✓ mannerisms
- ✓ way of walking

Hear Your Character Speaking

Tune in and listen to your character speaking. Notice his or her

- ✓ manner of speaking
- ✓ unusual use of words
- ✓ accent or dialect

Examine All the Aspects of Your Character

Think of this character as a real person—someone you used to know. Reflect on his or her

- ✓ life-style
- ✓ relationships
- ✓ essential nature
- ✓ mode of operation
- ✓ world view

152   *Reading / People on Pages*

Look Inside Your Character's Head

Tune into what is going on inside your character's head. What are his or her

- ✓ habits of thought
- ✓ inconsistencies between thoughts and actions
- ✓ desires
- ✓ strong passions concealed from others

Visualize Your Character in a Full Scene

You can recreate one from the story itself or make up your own.

- ✓ What does this scene reveal most about your character?
- ✓ How is this scene a typical one for your character?

✍ COMPLETING THE EXPERIENCE

- ✓ Write down a quick list of all the words you associate with your character.

- ✓ In about 100 words, write a portrait of your character. Describe the one major quality which you think best explains him or her.

✍ WRITING FROM THE EXPERIENCE

- ✓ Describe your character in action in the scene you visualized above. Be certain to build to a climactic interest and show why the scene is important and what it reveals about your character.

- ✓ Imagine you are having a conversation with this person about your life. Write down what you think he or she would tell you. What advice could you get from this character?

- ✓ In your journal, conduct an exploration of all the character's traits which you would like to own. Name the traits, justify them, and explain why you would like to have them for yourself. What would you do if you had these same traits? How would your life be different?

✍ GOING FURTHER

E.M. Forster in *Aspects of the Novel* says that there's a difference between people in books and people in daily life:

> In daily life we never understand each other, neither complete clairvoyance nor complete confessional exists. We know each other approximately, by external

signs, and these serve well enough as a basis for society and even for intimacy. But people in a novel can be understood completely by the reader, if the novelist wishes; their inner as well as their outer life can be exposed. And this is why they often seem more definite than characters in history, or even our own friends.

—E.M. Forster
Aspects of the Novel

✓ Choose one character from literature (you can use the one in your exercise) and, applying Forster's above idea, undertake a thorough study of both the character's inner and outer life. Write a paper in which you introduce the character as a person outside the novel or short story—as a real or historical person. In the first half of the paper, describe the character's outer life—his or her circumstances, strivings, or mode of operation. In the second half of the paper, bring in all you know or can surmise about the character's invisible life—his or her passions, secret thoughts, schemes, repressed impulses, and so forth. The challenge will then be to try to bring these two halves together into a strong unified statement at the end which will cause the reader of your paper to agree with you.

✓ Show this character in action. Enlist help from a couple of friends or undertake a group project with others where you will all work together to help each other present character scenes. Select a few scenes from the novel or story that you think are most revealing about your character. Decide on the major statement you want to make about the character and select the scenes accordingly. You take the lead role and assign friends supporting roles. Write out a script and rehearse, then present the scenes to the class or a group. The addition of some props, bits of costumes, poster boards with key information, and so forth can add a lot. If you're really inspired, you can videotape the scene sequence, add some music, and then present it to the class.

Exercise 4
Reading
A FAVORITE AUTHOR REVISITED

A favorite author is like an old friend—someone you can sit down with and feel immediately at home again, even after a long absence. Sometimes favorite authors get put on the shelf for awhile, or they get replaced with other favorites, or they disappear without our even noticing they've gone until years later. Here's a chance for you to revisit some of those authors you might have loved and lost.

Make a Mental List of Authors You Especially Like

These can be authors you are currently reading and those you remember from your past.

Close Your Eyes and Mentally See Some of the Books

Take several deep breaths, close your eyes, and visualize several of the books by different authors. If you know what the author looks like, visualize him or her also.

Go Back in Time to an Early Age

Visualize yourself getting younger and younger. Return to a time in your early childhood when you loved a particular author's books. Vividly remember yourself looking at and reading these books—or having them read to you.

- ✓ What do you love best about these books?
- ✓ What impact do they have on your imagination?

Travel Forward Through the Years and Remember Other Authors

See yourself growing up, reading different books. Remember particular authors that you especially liked. Take enough time to go through your life so that you can recall authors and books you may have forgotten about.

- ✓ Which books stand out most vividly?
- ✓ Which books are written by the same author?

Recollect Specific Books You Have Read Recently

Visualize yourself traveling forward and coming into the last two or three years. Remember some of the books you have read and recall the authors of those books.

Now Focus on One Particular Author That You Especially Like

This author can be from the present time or from your past. Take time to recall each book you have read by this author. Also remember the titles of other books by this same author which you have not yet read.

- ✓ What is most outstanding about this author's style?
- ✓ What common themes do you usually find in this author's books?

Recall Your Favorite Book by This Author

Remember your favorite book by this author and visualize yourself reading it:

✓ Where are you? What is going on in your life at this time?
✓ What caused you to read this particular book?
✓ What impact does it have on you?
✓ What do you like most about it?

Think About Why You Like This Author

Think now about the author and what you like specifically about him or her.

✓ What stands out most for you about this author?
✓ How has this author influenced your thinking?

✎ WRITING WARM-UP

✓ Write down the name of your author and all the titles of his or her books that you can remember.

✓ In a few sentences, sum up why this author stands out in your mind.

✎ WRITING ABOUT THE EXPERIENCE

✓ Write a brief history of your relationship with this author and his or her books. Emphasize the most important book and explain the influence the author has had on you.

✓ Write a paper about this author, giving your own point of view about his or her outstanding qualities as a writer. Back up what you say with evidence from the books whenever possible. Make this paper an introduction to the author in which you will persuade your reader that this writer is worth reading.

✎ EXPANDING THE EXPERIENCE

✓ Locate one or more books by your author and look through them. Jot down all the things you notice about the author's style of writing. Then choose one short passage that you particularly like and study it closely. Read the passage aloud a couple of times to hear the rhythm of the sentences. Next copy the passage over in your own handwriting. Take enough time to get the feel of the writer's words into your own fingertips. Now begin your own passage of writing, using your author's sentences as a starting point. Consciously imitate the sentence patterns and your author's tone and voice, but use your own words and ideas. Once you've finished a paragraph or so of imitation, keep going with your own composition. Move beyond the imitation into your own creation and see what happens. You might find yourself writing something totally unexpected, something quite unusual for you as a writer. Expect to do so.

Choose one idea that you got from this author. This can be an idea which he or she repeats in several books or it can be an idea you got from one book. Keep in mind that a lot of reading happens between the lines—you, the reader, often will fill in details, ideas, or thoughts. So it is possible that you obtained your idea in an indirect way from this author and that's fine also. Do a freewrite in which you set down everything you know and think about this idea. Then conduct an inquiry into the history of this idea:

✓ Where did it first come from?
✓ How long has it been around?
✓ What people or groups of people are associated with it?
✓ How has it changed over the years?
✓ What impact has it had on the world and/or people?

A fascinating source with which to start your research is a five-volume reference work: *Dictionary of the History of Ideas: Studies of the Selected Pivotal Ideas*, Philip P. Wiener, Editor-in-Chief. Nearly every major concept, ideology, idea, practice, and so forth is discussed in essays followed by valuable bibliographies at the end of each of them.

✓ Write a paper in which you set forth this idea as an influential force. Trace the history of it, showing the transformations it has gone through, and bring it up to date. Be sure to include as illustrations your author and your own experiences. End by emphasizing what effect this idea has on the world today.

✓ You can also write a paper in which you attack this idea as a lie or an illusion. This will take some work, especially if you believe in the idea. You are going to take arms against it deliberately, just for the experience of arguing objectively against an idea that is important to you. End your paper with suggestions for how this idea could be wiped out. Don't be afraid to try a bit of humor here if it seems appropriate.

✓ Undertake a thorough study of your author's literary accomplishments. Locate books and articles that give assessments and interpretations of the author's works and do some general reading. Freewrite to discover your own slant on the subject: What do you feel is the most outstanding accomplishment of your author? Write a paper that explains and defends your main idea. Use examples, both from the author's works and from the critics, to prove your point.

Chapter 14

—————— MIND PLAY ——————

There is nothing either good or bad, but thinking makes it so.

—Shakespeare
Hamlet

Mind play is not only fun; it also expands your thinking powers. In these exercises you'll have a chance to give your mind a workout. Some of the exercises will help you gain greater concentration and inventiveness; others will help you see things in a new way. The following exercises are in this chapter:

- *A Five-Minute Concentration Exercise*
- *Dreaming Up an Invention*
- *Repeat Performance*
- *Sex Change*

Exercise 1 A FIVE-MINUTE CONCENTRATION
Mind Play EXERCISE

One of the first steps to setting your mind free is training it to concentrate at will. By commanding your mind to stay focused on one idea for a set period of time, you can improve your mental flexibility and open up pathways in your thinking and creativity.

Set at a Desk with Pen and Paper Handy

Sit up in a straight chair, preferably at a desk, and have pen and paper at hand. Take several deep breaths, and as you exhale, relax your body more with each exhale.

Choose a Small Object That Is Not in the Room to Concentrate On

The object should be small enough to hold in your hands. *Choose an object that is not in the room with you.* The idea is to build up the image in your mind as concretely as possible.

Time Your Concentration Period for Five Minutes

Set a timer, or keep a clock where you can see it, and limit your concentration period to five minutes.

Begin Concentrating on the Object You've Chosen

As you concentrate, *keep your eyes open* and find a comfortable spot on the floor to focus on. Begin to visualize your object in as much detail as possible. Do not write yet.

Take Your Concentration Through Three Levels

You don't have to try all three levels; it's better to fully accomplish the first one before moving to the next. However, if you feel that you want to try all three, you can move your concentration from the concrete to the abstract through these three levels:

Concrete Physical Characteristics First build up the physical aspects of your object—its shape, size, weight, color, and texture. Really visualize it and experience things about it you may not have noticed before. What are some of its most distinguishing characteristics?

Practical Aspects of the Object Consider the practical aspects of this object.

- ✓ How is it used?
- ✓ Where does it come from?
- ✓ How does it get to us?
- ✓ Who invented it?
- ✓ What are all the different ways it could be used?

Abstract Considerations Speculate on the deeper meaning of your object.

- ✓ Why do we value this object?
- ✓ How has it changed historically?
- ✓ What is its place in today's world?
- ✓ What does it symbolize to us?

Simultaneously Observe Your Own Mental Processes

As you concentrate, notice how your mind works. Pay attention to both the quality and the focus of your concentration. When you catch your mind wandering, bring it back to your object. Make a small mark each time your mind wanders during the exercise so that you can get a concrete idea of how long you are able to will your mind to concentrate.

✍ WRITING WARM-UP

✓ As soon as the exercise is over, write a paragraph evaluating your ability to concentrate. Total up the number of marks you made when your mind wandered. Were you able to catch yourself quickly and return to the concentration or did your mind slip out the window and never come back? Be honest. The more clearly you see your mind at work, the better chance you have of taming it when you want to.

✓ Write down a brief description of the object and indicate if you were surprised by anything new you discovered about it. Add a drawing of it if you'd like to.

✍ WRITING ABOUT THE EXPERIENCE

✓ Write a short paper about the object itself. Include all you thought of, the questions raised, the physical details of the object. Include as much information as you can about the object on all three levels: the physical, the practical use of it, the abstract or symbolic meanings of it. You can add these now, even if you were unable to get through all three levels during the exercise. (Be sure to describe the object physically in detail so your reader can see it.)

Think of your relationship to this object. Why did you choose it? The French philosopher, Gaston Bachelard, says

> We have only to speak of an object to think that we are being objective. But, because we chose it in the first place, the object reveals more about us than we do about it.
>
> —Gaston Bachelard
> *The Psychoanalysis of Fire*

✓ Write a journal entry in which you explore your connection with this particular object. Don't be satisfied with a simple explanation. Dig down and find out why your mind chose this object. What deeper meaning might this object have for you?

✍ EXPANDING THE EXPERIENCE

✓ Get together with a group of friends or classmates and practice the exercise. Choose a common object that everyone in the group will concentrate on. Set a timer. When the time is up, let everyone write for ten minutes about the object. Then read aloud and compare the information that emerges. Afterward, each participant should write up a report of the experiment and evaluate the group's success in concentrating. Include in the report all new information the group discovered about the object through this process.

✓ Use this same five-minute concentration technique (you can expand it to ten or fifteen minutes when you're able) to concentrate in depth on a news item which you can randomly choose from the front page of the newspaper. After using it again on your own, write a progress report evaluating how well you did and compare it to the first time you did the exercise. What did you discover? What value did you gain by focusing your concentration on this event? Also include in your report all the information you thought of during the five minutes.

Exercise 2
Mind Play
DREAMING UP AN INVENTION

At one time or another you have probably said, "Why haven't they ever invented a _____?" Usually that statement grows out of frustration over an unmet need. Now you get a chance to invent an item you've always wanted by have never found on the shelves.

Give Yourself a 15-Minute Concentration Period to Recall Any Past Ideas You've Had for an Invention

Keep your eyes open throughout a 15-minute period of concentration but focus on one spot so you don't get distracted. Keep a pad and pen handy. Think back over times in the past when you've felt frustrated because you needed or wanted an object that simply did not exist. Perhaps you had to put together a make-do object in order to get the job done. If several ideas occur to you, pick one to work with and go directly to visualizing the object. If no ideas occur to you:

Think of an activity you know well and take yourself through each step of it: Go through the action from start to finish and don't leave out any of the steps.

Find some step in the activity that could be improved by the use of a new gadget: If you can't think of a brand-new gadget to invent, think of a slight improvement. How would you explain to someone else the way this gadget or improvement could help?

Visualize the Object in as Much Detail as Possible

At this point you might want to close your eyes so you can see the object more vividly. Watch the object in action until you find yourself creating more physical details for it.

Now See Yourself Using the New Invention

Go through the activity mentally again, this time *with* the object you've thought of. You are now well on your way to inventing a new thingamajig.

Look at the Individual Parts of the Object

Examine the parts of the object carefully.

- ✓ What are they made of?
- ✓ How are they put together?
- ✓ How do they work individually?
- ✓ How do they work together?

What Will This Invention Do for Others?

Think about how the average consumer could use this object.

- ✓ What is its purpose?
- ✓ Who will use it?
- ✓ How will it make life easier for others?
- ✓ What gap will it fill—or what object will it replace?

How Could This Object Be Manufactured or Otherwise Created?

Consider further how this object is made.

- ✓ What are the materials necessary for creating this invention?
- ✓ By what process could it be put together?
- ✓ What would it cost?

✍ WRITING WARM-UP

- ✓ You might have made a few notes or doodles on your pad. Now draw a quick sketch—any kind you can manage—and label the parts. Then write down everything you imagined as rapidly as possible. Don't worry about being logical or precise. Simply get as much down as you can so that your ideas don't evaporate.

✓ Write an advertising slogan for your invention. What market will you aim for? Where will your ad appear?

✍ WRITING ABOUT THE EXPERIENCE

✓ Now put your ideas into a more organized form. Take the material you've written above and expand it. Now's the time to write down in detail a full description of your invention and all the ideas you have about it. Take this task seriously, as if your invention will really exist at a future date.

✓ Create a full marketing plan for your invention. This doesn't have to be a genuine marketing plan; just put down all your ideas for the invention.

✓ Who will be the primary users of this object?
✓ How will others be able to buy it?
✓ What gap will it fill?
✓ How will you finance it?

✍ EXPANDING THE EXPERIENCE

Although this exercise is intended primarily to increase your creative thinking powers, it's quite possible that you will at some point come up with an invention you think is a winner. If you are willing to invest your time, energy, and money in it, there are many societies for inventors where you can find people to help you develop your idea and even make a model of it.

✓ There are numerous books out there on how to create and sell inventions and most of the books give you all the information you need to get started. They include practical advice as well as names and addresses of pertinent organizations. Do some research on what it takes to own an invention—from patent to final product. Write a paper explaining your invention and what steps you would have to take in order to make it a reality.

✓ Choose an invention that intrigues you. Keep in mind that just about everything you use today—key chains, post-it notes, frisbees, hair spray, staplers—was once an idea in someone's head which later became a commercial venture. Concentrate on a small invention so you won't become overwhelmed with information. Write a history of this one invention, tracing its progress from its earliest beginnings to today. Use illustrations when appropriate to show the different forms it has taken. An excellent source book to help you get started is *The Picture History of Inventions* by Umberto Eco and G. B. Zorzoli.

Repeat Performance

A popular form of mental play is reliving the past—hoping this time it will turn out different. If you have some events in your life that you wish had turned out differently, here's an exercise that will let you rewrite them to your specifications.

Select an Event in Your Past That You'd Like to Change

It can be a dramatic event—something with a strong emotional charge—or a minor event which, for some reason, keeps replaying in your memory for a reason you might not understand.

Replay the Event in Your Imagination

Close your eyes for a few moments and let the event unfold, from beginning to end, in your mind's eye.

- ✓ Where does it take place?
- ✓ Who are the people involved? Is anyone missing who had an impact on the event?
- ✓ What is your role in this event? What are your thoughts and feelings?
- ✓ How does it end?

Allow the Memory to Dissolve, and Think It Through Again

Open your eyes and consciously run through the process briefly so that all the details are arranged firmly in your mind.

Now Close Your Eyes and Start the Event Over

Visualize the event from start to finish again, this time in slow motion. Watch the action closely as it progresses so that you can pinpoint the turning point which could change the outcome.

Interrupt the Action and Send It in a New Direction

When the action reaches the turning point, interrupt it and send it in the direction you choose. Stay with it until you have the events going just the way you want them to go.

Let the Action Continue Until You Reach a Full Resolution

Keep going until you feel completely satisfied and have the ending you have always wanted for this event. Enjoy your success.

Open Your Eyes and See How You Feel

Check in with yourself and see how you feel about having changed the outcome of this event. Mentally review and compare the two endings. How different are they?

———————◼———————

✍ WRITING WARM-UP

✓ Write a sentence describing how you feel now.

✓ Sum up in a few sentences how you changed the ending and why.

✍ WRITING ABOUT THE EXPERIENCE

✓ Narrate the event twice—once the way it actually turned out and then write how you recreated it. Compare the two endings and include your own observations and any discoveries you made during the process. How much do the two endings differ? Does changing the ending make a big or small difference in the event for you?

✓ Write a journal entry concentrating on how you feel about the actual event and explain why you wanted to change the ending. Describe your feelings about it now that you've changed the ending. Did you discover anything new about yourself? If so, include that also.

✍ EXPANDING THE EXPERIENCE

The title for this exercise came from a 1947 movie, *Repeat Performance*, staring Joan Leslie and Louis Hayward. At the end of a troubled, traumatic year, the central character (played by Joan Leslie) discovers that she's been given a chance to live the year over. She's certain she can make it turn out differently now that she knows what is going to happen. But as the events begin to unfold, she finds she is helpless to change their course. No matter what she does, the events manage to circumvent any new action and proceed toward their natural conclusion. At the end, of course, all the major events turn out exactly as they did the year before. They, too, got a "repeat performance."

The theme of fate is often explored in film and literature. This 200-word short story, "An Appointment in Samarra" by W. Somerset Maugham, is one of the most famous illustrations of this theme.

There was a merchant in Bagdad who sent his servant to market to buy provisions, and in a little while the servant came back, white and trembling, and said, "Master, just now when I was in the market-place I was jostled by a woman in the crowd and when I turned I saw it was Death that jostled me. She looked at me and made a threatening gesture; now, lend me your horse, and I will ride away from this city and avoid my fate. I will go to Samarra and there Death will not find me." The merchant lent him his horse, and the servant mounted it, and he dug his spurs in its flanks and as fast as the horse could gallop he went. Then the merchant went down to the market-place and he saw Death standing in the crowd and he came to Death and said, "Why did you make a threatening gesture to my servant when you saw him this morning?" "That was not a threatening gesture," Death said. "It was only a start of surprise. I was astonished to see him in Bagdad, for I had an appointment with him tonight in Samarra."

—W. Somerset Maugham
"An Appointment in Samarra"

✓ Respond to Maugham's short story. Study the structure of it, paying close attention to each sentence. What do each one of them contribute to the story? Write between the lines: After each sentence, fill in other details with your imagination. What is left out? What else might have been included? Now write your own version of this story. You can change certain elements (such as setting), but keep Maugham's basic structure. Make your own story a restatement and expanded version of Somerset Maugham's. Be certain that the theme of fate comes through clearly in your story.

✓ Think about the idea of fate. What do you really believe about this? Do you agree that life and events are fated and that we as human beings actually have no control or say so about what will happen? This question is deeply philosophical, so don't be too quick to come up with an answer. Instead, write a paper in which you explore your ideas and feelings and discover what you actually do believe. After you've used your writing to discover your ideas and feelings, then you can put them together in a more organized paper which gives your views about the role fate plays in life.

✓ Rewriting endings to novels, movies, plays, and short stories is a great way to stimulate your imagination and expand your creativity. Choose a piece of literature you have always wanted to turn out differently and rewrite the ending as you imagine it. You can either change the ending as it was written or continue the ending and take it in a different direction, but be certain that your ending is plausible. Also, try to retain the writer's style and voice as much as possible when you write your own piece. (If rewriting the ending to a piece of literature doesn't interest you, you can rewrite the ending to an historical event.)

Exercise 4
Mind Play

SEX CHANGE

Surely you've thought about how it would feel to be the other sex. Now here's your chance to get a feeling of what you might be like had you been born that opposite sex. If possible, have a friend or your teacher guide you through this exercise.

Close Your Eyes and Visualize Yourself from Head to Foot the Way You Are Now

Take a few moments to breathe deeply. Become very aware of your body and its sensations. Slowly visualize yourself from head to foot exactly as you are right now. Don't move your imagination from a body part until you've gotten a vivid picture of it in your mind.

Imagine Yourself Waking Up in Bed on a Sunny Morning

You awake and start to stretch. Everything seems to be the same—same bed, same bedroom. You think for a moment about what you did the night before.

You Slowly Realize That Something About You Is Different

You can tell, even before you open your eyes, that something is different. In fact something is *very* different. You lie there with your eyes closed, still half asleep, trying to get the sense of what is going on. Gradually you begin to realize that something about your body has changed.

You Discover That You Have Had a Sex Change

You run your hands over your body and a shock ripples through you. You can't take it in all at once. You open your eyes and look at yourself: Somehow or other during the night, your sex has changed.

You Go to the Mirror and Look at Your New Body

You look with amazement at your body in the mirror. You're still the same person. Nothing has changed about you emotionally or mentally. But physically you have become a member of the opposite sex. Take in all the physical changes that have occurred in your body. Look at every new feature you now have.

Let the Story Unfold However You Like

Once you've got a clear sense of the new you, let the story go in any direction you like.

- ✓ What happens next?
- ✓ Who else is in the house with you?
- ✓ How do you handle this change?
- ✓ Where do you go from here? What do you do?
- ✓ How do other people react to you?

✐ WRITING WARM-UP

- ✓ Give yourself a name for when you were the opposite sex. Now briefly describe what you looked like and how it felt to be the other gender.

- ✓ Write a journal entry in which you explore your response to the exercise. What was it like for you? How well did you do with it?

✐ WRITING ABOUT THE EXPERIENCE

Before you begin writing about your experience, think about these questions. If you were suddenly the opposite sex:

- ✓ How would you genuinely feel about it?
- ✓ What kind of person would you be?
- ✓ What knowledge that you now have would be useful to you?
- ✓ How would being the opposite sex change the way you do things?

- ✓ Write a paper in which you present the experience of the exercise first; then carry your discussion into more general terms: Address the insights you've gained about the opposite sex and how these insights might affect your future actions.

- ✓ A natural paper from this experience would be a fantasy which continues the exercise. Write a narrative which recreates the experience and then keep going. Imagine that, after you've discovered your sex change in your own home, you now go outside and meet others who know you.

✍ EXPANDING THE EXPERIENCE

✓ Now that you've had the experience of being the opposite gender, you can use what you've gained to do serious exploration into some of the ongoing issues between the sexes. Plan for a small group discussion; be certain that it's gender-balanced, such as three females and three males. Discuss your gripes against the opposite sex. Allow the opposite side to reply. After the discussion, pick one issue which has been a problem for you personally with members of the opposite sex. Make it as specific as possible. Set out to learn all you can about this problem from the view of the opposite sex. Put your views aside for now. You want to see the issue from the other side of the fence. Deliberately read literature that presents information from the opposite view—for example, if you are male, read literature that promotes the female point of view and vice versa. For a humorous look at a sex change, see the movie *Switch*. After you've done some thoughtful exploration of the issue, write a paper in which you discuss the issue and offer possible solutions.

✓ Take this topic all the way home: Do a historical study of the war between the sexes. What exactly is the "war between the sexes?" Give it some thought before you start doing any further reading about it. First do a couple of freewrites about your feelings about the situation. Next meet with a few friends (of both sexes) and discuss it. After these activities, some questions will occur to you that you will want to have answered. At that point, undertake some historical study and find the thread that interests you most. Write a paper in which you outline one particular aspect of the conflict between the sexes and trace its development, illuminating the causes and effects. End your paper with an assessment of where we stand now.

Chapter 15

—————— IMAGINATION ——————

Look, I made a hat . . .
Where there never was a hat . . .

—Stephen Sondheim
"Finishing the Hat"

Imaginings can sometimes take us over and cause us trouble—as in imagining forthcoming disasters, excessive daydreaming, circular conversations in our head, living in fantasies, and so forth. In these cases, the imagination has us. But for *us* to have our imagination and use it as we choose—ah, that can be heaven. Nothing is more important to a writer than a strong and active imagination that can be used as a conscious tool for the craft of writing. See what your imagination brings you from the following exercises:

- *Whisper*
- *You Are the Camera*
- *Empty Stage*
- *A Nightmare*

Exercise 1
Imagination WHISPER

Listening in on other people's conversations, especially if they sound full of emotion and meaning, is usually irresistible. No matter what's being said, we find ourselves filling in the blanks and coming up with our own scenario for what's going on. This exercise asks you to imagine listening in on a conversation between two people and then write down what you hear.

Imagine Yourself in a Public Setting

Close your eyes and imagine yourself in a public setting—a restaurant, a park, an elevator, a bus, or a mall. Take time to create the details of the place.

Imagine You Hear Two People Nearby Whispering to Each Other

You see two strangers nearby engaged in an intense private conversation. They don't know that you are observing them because they are too absorbed in their conversation.

Take a Look at Each of the People

Notice what each of the people looks like.

- ✓ What do you surmise about them and their relationship?
- ✓ What do you imagine their lives are like?
- ✓ What is the current situation that has led to the conversation?
- ✓ What are they doing as they talk?

Listen to Their Conversation

Now listen in on what they are saying as they whisper to each other. Remember: This is a private conversation and you are eavesdropping. They are completely unaware of you.

- ✓ Record the dialogue between them as accurately as possible. Give yourself enough time and space for the conversation to unfold completely.
- ✓ Try to capture the cadence, accent, and unusual expressions of each person's speech.

Make Up a Story About Them

As you listen to them whisper:

- ✓ What is the story that goes on in your head about these two people?
- ✓ What can you tell about them after you have heard them talking?
- ✓ What do you think happens after this conversation?

———■———

✐ WRITING WARM-UP

- ✓ Assess your response to the exercise. How vividly were you able to imagine the scene? Could you actually hear the people's voices? In a couple of sentences, explain whether the exercise worked for you—and explain why or why not.

  - ✓ Write a brief description of the two characters, their relationship, and the setting.

✍ WRITING ABOUT THE EXPERIENCE

✓ Write down the conversation exactly as you heard it. Try to capture the distinct flavor of each person's manner of speaking. Put the conversation into correct dialogue form, indicating who is speaking when necessary. Also add bits of description and explanation for clarification.

Here's a brief passage of dialogue, which you can study for form, from F. Scott Fitzgerald's short story, "Babylon Revisited." A father and his nine-year-old daughter, who does not live with him, are having lunch together in a restaurant.

"I want to get to know you," he said gravely. "First let me introduce myself. My name is Charles J. Wales, of Prague."

"Oh, daddy!" her voice cracked with laughter.

"And who are you please?" he persisted and she accepted a role immediately: "Honoria Wales, Rue Palatina, Paris."

"Married or single?"

"No, not married. Single."

He indicated the doll. "But I see that you have a child, madame."

✓ After you have written down the conversation between your characters, take your writing a step further and create a story about these two people. Who are they? What's at stake right at this moment? Write a few paragraphs explaining their story. Incorporate the dialogue you wrote if appropriate.

✍ EXPANDING THE EXPERIENCE

✓ Continue the action of the story by writing a full scene that shows what happens next. What happens to these two people after they leave? Build your scene out of the relationship you have established between them: Give your scene a setting, add dialogue and description, and let something important happen.

✓ To go further in creating characters and dialogue, try this idea: Cut out half a dozen photographs of real people (not models in ads) from different magazines. Or locate books of fine photographs of people. An outstanding book of such photographs (417 of them) is *Fellini's Faces* by Christian Strich. Choose a character who attracts your interest and put the picture before you. Examine it closely. Begin to imagine the kind of life this person has, the type of person he or she is. What does this person want? Put yourself into a receptive frame of mind and imagine the character speaking directly to you. Let this other voice say

Imagination 173

whatever it wants to while you record what it is saying. Write up the story this voice tells you. Another option would be to take two or three of the photographs and imagine a scene among the characters and then write down what you imagined.

Exercise 2
Imagination

YOU ARE THE CAMERA

In this exercise, you are the camera, recording the scene that takes place before you. You're going to first dress the set with scenery, people, and objects and then watch and record the scene that develops. If possible, have your teacher or a friend take you through the exercise. Otherwise, read through the whole exercise first to get ready because you'll be working with your eyes closed most of the time.

Study This List or Have It Read to You

You can memorize this list or have someone read it to you—or open your eyes when necessary.

- ✓ A green bottle
- ✓ An oak table
- ✓ A woman in white
- ✓ Two men
- ✓ A lawnmower
- ✓ Sunlight

Close Your Eyes and Pretend That You Are a Camera

Feel the darkness around you as if you are the inside of a camera. As a camera, you will objectively observe and record what you see.

Visualize the Items One at a Time

Give yourself space between items so that each one can "arrange" itself where it wants to be. After you've placed the items, including characters, into relationship with one another, pan the entire scene as a movie camera does.

Allow the People and Objects to Come to Life

Let the scene come to life any way it chooses.

Watch the Scene Unfold, and Mentally Record What You See and Hear

Allow the scene to unfold fully. Don't rush it—relax and let the action go on as long as it likes or until you feel you have taken everything in that you want to. Let the characters and objects surprise you. Have some fun.

See if One of the Characters Dominates the Scene

If a character wants to take over the scene, let it do so. Follow this character's lead and see what happens.

Let the Scene End

After a few more minutes, let the scene dissolve. Open your eyes, but before you begin to write, replay the scene in your imagination. You may find yourself adding details and ideas and developing the action further.

———————————■———————————

✍ WRITING WARM-UP

✓ Write a few sentences assessing your participation in this exercise. Were you able to imagine a scene in which a strong action happened? How vivid was it? Did you relinquish control and allow the objects and characters to move freely?

✓ In a short paragraph, briefly describe the scene and then explain whether or not you were surprised by the outcome of the scene.

✍ WRITING FROM THE EXPERIENCE

✓ Write the scene as you saw it. Let the characters come to life on paper. *Show* the scene happening.

✓ Now go a step further: What happens after the scene ends? Narrate what you imagine happening next.

✓ Tell a story from the point of view of one of the characters or objects—the lawnmower, for example.

✍ EXPANDING THE EXPERIENCE

✓ Now that you've had experience in allowing a scene to come to life, do the exercise again and write another, perhaps more detailed, scene. Your inner eye should be even more vivid now. Here are three other lists which you can use to create other scenes. However, to develop your maximum creativity through this exercise, you should begin to make up your own objects and characters. As you progress, you can take more risks and make some of your scenes offbeat—even absurd. Try this exercise with a small group and take turns leading the visualization. Have fun making up your own lists.

- *An apple*
- *Rain*
- *A child*
- *A hat*
- *Three adults*
- *A clothespin*

- *An elderly couple*
- *A forest*
- *A radio*
- *A piece of paper*
- *Strong wind*
- *An animal*

- *A pair of sneakers*
- *The ocean*
- *A car*
- *Two teenagers*
- *Heat*
- *A clock*

✓ To give your creativity further stimulation, try the following technique: Cut out a group of photographs from a variety of magazines. Then cut out the object or person or scenery that interests you most from each photograph and discard the rest of the photograph. Next arrange these cutouts into some sort of still life (you should have at least six to ten items). Observe the new picture you have created with these unconnected items and let your imagination suggest a scene. At this point, you can close your eyes and allow the scene to start rolling—but you might find that the visual stimulation of your put-together picture is enough to trigger sufficient material. Write down the scene you imagine and then let it go as far as your imagination can take it.

Exercise 3
Imagination
EMPTY STAGE

The title itself gives you some idea of what you'll be doing in this exercise: peopling an empty stage with actors, scenery, and props and then setting them into action. This gives you another approach to creating dramatic scenes out of your own head.

If you can actually put yourself in front of an empty stage—a school auditorium or a small playhouse—that's fine. Most likely you will be creating everything, including the empty stage, with your imagination—and that's just as good.

Close Your Eyes and Imagine an Empty Stage

You've no doubt seen many different stages in your life. Just visualize any kind of stage you can remember.

Imagine Yourself Seated in the Audience, Watching the Stage

In your imagination, put yourself into the audience in front of an empty stage.

Place a Few Props Around the Stage

Slowly begin to set a scene by imagining a few props. Keep the furnishings and props as simple as possible, but choose objects that can be used in an interesting way.

Light the Stage

Watch the lights on the stage come up. Take enough time to get exactly the quality of light you want on the stage. Vary the tints and shadings until you have created precisely the atmosphere you want.

Bring Some Characters onto the Stage

You can people the stage with as few or as many characters as you like. Even one character will do. You might also start with a few characters and add others as you go along.

Start the Action in the Middle of the Play

Begin the action and watch it unfold. This is not the beginning of the play. Other scenes and action have taken place before this moment.

✓ What has happened prior to this?
✓ What is going on right at this moment?

Let the Characters Speak

Listen to the dialogue (or monologue) that is going on. Stay with this awhile until you hear real people talking.

✓ What is each of the characters saying?
✓ To whom is each character speaking?

Observe Each of the Characters in Detail

Use your imagination to develop each of the characters into real human beings.

✓ What do each of them look like?
✓ What is each doing?
✓ What are some of their unusual mannerisms?
✓ What do each of them want? What is at stake?

Turn Off the Lights

End the scene by darkening the stage.

✓ What was the main effect of this scene?
✓ What idea, image, or atmosphere lingers after the scene is over?
✓ What do you think will happen next?

✍ WRITING WARM-UP

✓ Write *three* sentences: One which fully explains the beginning of the scene; another which tells the main action in the scene; and a third sentence which tells what happened at the end.

✓ Imagine what the next scene will be. Which direction would you like the story to go? Write a brief summary of what you think should happen next.

✍ WRITING FROM THE EXPERIENCE

✓ Write the scene out as you saw it in as much detail as possible. (Keep in mind what you know will happen next, but don't give it away in this scene. Use the knowledge to create tension and suspense.) Create the scene entirely with dialogue and stage directions. If you need help with the play format, get a play and see how it is arranged on the page.

✓ Now write a second scene—the one you imagined above that would come next. Work for continuity between the two scenes as much as possible. In writing these scenes, you don't have to make absolute sense. You are working primarily to experiment with dramatic structure, dialogue, and character development.

✍ EXPANDING THE EXPERIENCE

✓ Get together a few friends or classmates in order to hear the scenes read out loud. This is an essential step in working on the dialogue. Make copies of your scenes and bring them to the group. Assign each of the roles to different members of the group and have both scenes read out loud. While you're listening to the dialogue being spoken aloud, ask yourself, "Does this sound like real people talking?" "Would this character actually say this?" Make notes during the reading and later rewrite the scenes, incorporating any new ideas you got during the process. At some point, you might want to try your hand at writing a full one-act play.

✓ After the group has read all the scenes, now is a good time to study some one-act plays for structure and dialogue. For a large collection (40 plays), see *Plays in One Act* by Daniel Halpern. Have each member bring a recommendation and then select one which the group will study. Assign each person a role and begin reading the play aloud. Rotate the roles so that each member gets to read at least two different parts. Later, arrange a time when you can do a full reading of the play for either the class or another group. This doesn't have to be a big production, but a few props and some staging can add to the fun. If you're really inspired, you might make a home video which you can then show to the class. Note: An alternative to staging a one-act play would be to dramatize several scenes from a novel and present them. In this case, you might use a narrator to give the important information which takes place between the scenes.

Exercise 4
Imagination
A NIGHTMARE

Dreams, which come to us every night, are perpetual reminders of the depths of our imagination. Maybe you don't normally remember many of your dreams, but chances are you have had at least one nightmare in your life that you've never forgotten. Nightmares aren't necessarily full of evil people or monsters. They can portray a simple, everyday happening, which for some reason frightens you.

Pick a Nightmare You Vividly Remember

Choose one particular nightmare for this exercise. The nightmare can be a recent one or one from your childhood; it can be a recurring one or one you've had only once. Bring it briefly to mind before closing your eyes.

Now Close Your Eyes and Watch the Sequence of the Dream Unfold

Take several deep breaths to relax. Then begin to replay the dream. Watch it from start to finish as if it were a movie.

Go Back and Run It Through Again, Seeing It Moment by Moment

When you get to the end of the nightmare, go back and let it run through again. This time watch it as if it were a series of still photographs. Notice how you feel as you allow the dream to unfold without any resistance on your part.

Look Closely at All the Characters in the Dream

Focus first on the characters in your dream.

- ✓ Who are all the people in the dream? Don't leave anyone out.
- ✓ Where are *you* in the dream?
- ✓ Who is the central character in the dream other than yourself?
- ✓ Which character, if any, do you perceive as dangerous to you?
- ✓ Is anyone part of the dream who doesn't actually appear?

Get a Clear Picture of the Character or Characters Who Seem Dangerous to You

Let this character or characters grow and become even more threatening. Take a good look at your persecutor:

- ✓ What is the character doing to you or keeping you from doing?
- ✓ What is the most distinguishing feature of this character?
- ✓ What is most frightening to you?

Open Your Eyes and Think About the Sequence of the Dream Again

Now, with your eyes open, review the sequence of events in the dream:

- ✓ Where in your body do you feel the dream?
- ✓ Was anything or anybody part of the dream but outside the framework of the dream itself? If so, imagine what that missing part or character would be like.
- ✓ If you could put yourself in the place of the threatening character, how would you feel? What would you do?
- ✓ Were there any verbal or nonverbal messages given to you through the dream?

———■———

✐ WRITING WARM-UP

- ✓ Draw any kind of picture that symbolizes the scariest character or moment in the dream. Then write one sentence that explains your drawing.

- ✓ In a sentence or two, state what you think the message of the dream was for you. "I think this dream was trying to tell me. . . . "

✍ WRITING ABOUT THE EXPERIENCE

✓ Write a journal entry in which you explore the impact of this nightmare on you, both then and now. Has this dream occurred more than once in your life? If so, include how it has repeated itself over the years.

✓ Write the nightmare out like a simple story, beginning "Once upon a time. . . ." Turn it into a fairy tale or, if there are animals in it, into a fable. If you like, draw the dream in visual frames, step by step, like a comic strip, and add it to the end of your story.

✓ Write a fantasy in which you allow the most threatening character in the dream to become the central character. If this character could have its way, what would it do?

✓ Tell the missing part of the dream in detail—the part which took place offstage. What was going on elsewhere as the nightmare was unfolding? How were you aware of this?

✍ EXPANDING THE EXPERIENCE

Nightmares are usually the dreams we remember because they are so vivid and arouse intense feelings in us. But all of our dreams are important and can be meaningful to us. Learning to remember our dreams trains our memory as well as our imagination. Robert Bosnak, a dream analyst, says that

> Dreamwork is work on the imagination. . . . Especially in dreams it is clear how powerful the imagination is—it is capable of shaping a completely real world, indistinguishable from the physical world.

> —Robert Bosnak
> *A Little Course in Dreams*

The study of dreams, once considered by most of the Western world as of no consequence, became a serious branch of study with the publication of Sigmund Freud's *The Interpretation of Dreams* in 1900. Since then, as various branches of psychology have developed, dreams have taken a more central position as tools for understanding ourselves and our lives and there are now a mountain of books on the subject. While the theories of Sigmund Freud and Carl Jung still dominate most of the thinking about dreams, interest has increased in more esoteric dream work from other cultures. You can find numerous books on just about every aspect of dreams. A brief, fully illustrated book that will give you a good overview of various dream theories is *Dreams: Visions of the Night* by David Coxhead and Susan Hiller.

✓ Select a small group of friends or classmates with whom to share your dreams. Organize your discussion around one or two of these ideas:

✓ The nightmare you just experienced in the exercise

✓ Your earliest remembered childhood dream

✓ A recurring dream that still puzzles you

✓ A significant dream—one that changed you in some way

✓ A dream you've had in the past month

Once everyone has orally told a dream (keep the telling short—no more than two minutes apiece), then the group should start writing down the dreams as quickly as possible. First write your own dream—the one that seems most important. If there's still time, write down one other dream you heard in the group. Afterward, take time to share how it felt to reveal personal dreams and discuss any specific information learned from the discussion. Out of this discussion, questions should naturally arise about how to recall and interpret dreams. Follow up the discussion with some outside reading on this subject and then write a paper which explains what you found out. Use your own dreams and experiences as examples in the paper.

✓ If you are interested in going further with the subject of dreams, you can undertake an in-depth study of *one* of the major dream theories, such as the theories of Sigmund Freud or Carl Jung; or you can investigate older branches of dream work such as the Senoi Indians in Malaysia or the Iroquois Indians in America. The point is to focus very narrowly on one particular aspect, theory, or idea which intrigues you and then to study that in depth. If possible, interview an expert in your field of interest. Become knowledgeable in one tiny area of dream work and then present what you know in an informative paper. Be sure to place your information into a historical context—show where it fits in with the dream theory development.

Part V

GOING ON

Chapter 16

——— A FEW ESSENTIALS ———

Here we are on the other side of all those exercises and by now you've done a lot of writing and have already grappled with many of the essentials discussed in this chapter—may, in fact, have already used this chapter while writing papers. This is that kind of chapter, a come and go writer's reference section. It's here primarily to keep you reminded of some important ingredients necessary for putting your writing out there in the world.

VOICE

Every teacher has a pet hobbyhorse when it comes to writing. My own is voice. If a student's paper has a real voice, a strong one, I am usually a hooked reader no matter what other difficulties are in the paper. By voice I mean that I hear a real flesh-and-blood person talking directly to me, looking me in the eye, waiting for my response.

And when I write, the major starter for me is voice. I can't take a step until I get the voice that's going to write that particular piece. Most of the time I recognize that voice as one of my own many voices: the scared me, the schoolteacher me, the irreverent me, the carefree me, the angry me, and so on. These are voices I walk around with in my head all the time. But sometimes a voice I've never heard, a visitor I don't know, comes in and takes over my writing for awhile and leads me to some very exciting moments. When these people drop in and talk about themselves, I find myself writing things I never even thought of before.

You also have many different voices inside of you. At every minute of every day, there is a voice talking to you in your head. Some of these voices are you; others are voices of imaginary people. Your job as a writer is to become aware of all these voices, filter through them, and find the right one for each piece of writing you create.

Sometimes you will want to follow the imaginary voices. For example, one morning you might awaken and, as you're lying in bed, you hear a faint whisper in your head which says something like, "In the winter they always went to big cities to see the Christmas lights, four perfect blond children with their smiling mother and father." You might feel an urge to get out of bed and take down what the voice says and then continue following where it leads you. At these times you may find yourself writing poems, short stories, or other imaginative pieces.

Other times, probably the majority of times, you will be searching for the telling voice, the one which wants to give information to others. These will be the papers you write for classes or essays you hope to publish somewhere for others to read. The more voice you have in these papers, the easier the writing will flow from you and the more intensely it will be read by others. Voice, in fact, can make the difference in whether you succeed or fail with these papers, so keep trying out various voices until you hit on the perfect one for each paper.

If you're not yet aware of all the voice possibilities within you, go on a mining expedition and unearth some of these voices. You don't use only one voice when you speak, so don't lapse into the same old droning one when you write. Think for a moment of all the voices you use with different people in different situations. For example:

- your parents when they're vetoing your suggestions
- a salesperson who is trying to sell you something you don't want
- a teacher you can't stand
- your younger brother when he's asking too many questions
- a famous person you are meeting for the first time
- a close friend who is going through a hard time
- someone who might give you a job
- your heartthrob who has just called you long distance

To take this further, try an experiment: Write a short paragraph to three different people from the above list. If you're visualizing a real person as you talk, each of your three paragraphs will have a distinctly different voice.

And that's the way each paper you write should be. None of them should sound alike; yet all of them should sound like you.

AUDIENCE

Audience. Sometimes you have one and sometimes you don't. Sometimes you will write pieces simply because they want to be written for yourself. Other times you will be given an audience by a teacher, an editor, or a boss: "Tell the committee exactly what we expect to accomplish during the Hidigii Campaign." Sometimes you'll have an automatic audience—a poem written to someone you love, a letter to a friend. However, many times you will have *zero* audience. No audience whatsoever exists so far for this piece you are writing. But you write anyway and then you search for the audience. Professional writers do this all the time. They feel a burning need to write something, they write it, and then they set out to find an audience, sometimes years later.

In those times when the audience is hazy, the best thing to do for yourself is to make up an audience. Just mentally sit someone in a chair and talk away. Occasionally stop and let them ask you questions. This method always works if you trust in it and remember to do it. For example, as I am writing this, I am thinking of you. I have a rather mixed audience for this book—writers at all levels, students at all levels, many kinds of teachers who have different needs and goals . . . it gets intimidating. So what I do is imagine you. Sometimes you're a female, sometimes a male. Sometimes your hair is hanging over one eye or you're throwing paper balls in a trash can and half-listening to me. Sometimes you're in a chair in my room looking at me intently. Other times you're out in the garden and I have to call for you. But you are always some-where out there, making comments, asking questions, giving me ideas. That's audience. I made you up. You can do the same when you write. And, by the way, when you're making up your audience, be sure it's someone who likes you and thinks what you have to say is fascinating.

REVISION

In the next chapter, we will look at some specific revision techniques for turning a freewrite into an essay. But this section is about the *concept* of revision, of revision as a way of life forever after from this day forward. You have to buy the idea of revision right now and keep it burning brightly in your mind forevermore.

Nothing is ever really over, finished, done with. Even the past, which is supposedly an accomplished fact, continues to get decorated up and revised in our minds. People who are long gone from our lives keep presenting them-selves to us for conversation. A firm decision we made with strong conviction comes up later for a second look, for revision.

How then can writing, the lush profusion of our hearts and heads in one given moment, be any different? How can we expect to write something once and let it go without a second look? Yes, sometimes we experience that rare occurrence in writing when every word flows out and means what it says. But mostly we write, put it aside, rethink it, live with it awhile, and then revise. And revise.

And each revision has meaning for us. Each revision teaches us more and more about what we know, what we believe, what we feel, and what we are able to express. It's a mistake to think of a revision as menial labor, as some-thing to just get through. For each revision coaxes from us more material, asks that we bring more out of ourselves to it. Expect to revise constantly—and forever.

When you revise, you take another look at what you've written. Revision is the time you take to reconsider what you've written and make new decisions about it. Try to allow some time between writing and revising. After you've written a piece, put it away for at least a few hours before you sit down to revise it. When you revise, you may find yourself

- rethinking audience
- shifting tone

- adding many new details or paragraphs
- deciding to delete material as inappropriate
- rearranging material substantially
- adding new and deeper ideas which will give additional punch or meaning to what you've said
- making several new drafts
- writing new introductions and conclusions

An important concept to remember—and one that will keep you from getting bogged down and confused when you work—is that *writing* and *revising* are two separate activities. When you're writing, don't think about revising. The state of writing is usually rapid, exciting, creative, chaotic. It's very different from revision which is slow, organized, and methodical. Keep this distinction clear and, when you write, write without constraints. You'll write freer and easier knowing that revision is being set aside but will have its day later on.

INTRODUCTIONS, CONCLUSIONS, AND TITLES

These are all lumped together because they are three items that are often totally overlooked in the last minute rush of finishing a paper. So I put them here to remind you that all three of them are important and worth your best attention.

At the very moment when you are certain that you have finished your paper for good, stop and remember these three little words: *introduction, conclusion, title.* Go back one more time. Read your introduction and your conclusion. Do they do their jobs? Does the introduction grab the reader? Your introduction should pull your reader headlong into the essay. If you were reading your own paper, would you read past the introduction? And the conclusion—does it end with a strong punch? Or does it limp away? You have to leave your reader with something of substance at the end, some idea or statement that really leaves a mark. Otherwise, you have wasted your essay.

Then there's the title. This is the last item at the finish line and the one item that students are most apt to think the least of. A good title can not only announce specifically what your paper is about, but it can also add further meaning to your paper. Take time to come up with a good title—one that will invite and delight your reader.

CORRECTNESS

Correctness. That old bugaboo. All the while I've been telling you to forget correctness in the heat of writing. But eventually you must—everybody must—come back to it. Correctness counts too. Handing someone a paper to read that is full of errors wastes valuable time, both for yourself and the reader. In the first place, many of the errors could be careless ones—things you know better about (such as using "no" for "know" as I just did before I corrected it) but just haven't taken time to check over and correct. The second kind of error is one that you are totally unaware of and think, in fact, is correct as stands. For example, you might write, "That statement don't make any sense." The reader will mentally supply the correct verb form—"doesn't"—but will still struggle for a minute with whether you know better or not; in other words, such errors will take your reader away from the thoughts you're trying to get across. Then there are the other mistakes: garbled sentences, unclear statements that mean nothing to anyone—such as "the people who are responsible in the meantime for the better decision cannot be made alone." Getting on top of silly errors once and for all is easy enough to do: Buy yourself a good handbook, study it, keep it by your side, and consult it when in doubt.

The last two types of errors—the ones that the reader can make sense of even though grammatically incorrect and the ones that the reader can't make any sense of—are, surprisingly, not nearly the problem that *carelessness* is. In most of the papers I read, the majority of errors are not errors at all; they are simply glitches in the writer's attention and thinking. The writer knows better deep down but hasn't taken enough time to closely examine what's on the page. And that brings us to the next essential: proofreading.

PROOFREADING

Nothing saves the day—and your face—like proofreading. No matter how brilliant your paper is, if it's not proofread, you've lost a lot of luster because you're sure to have some unintentional errors. Proofreading and editing are not the same activities, though they often go on at the same time. Sometimes this can be a mistake. If you're trying to make even slight editorial decisions (like a change of word or phrase), this could distract you from the hard-nosed determination required for proofreading. Here are four steps to becoming a true proofreader:

- First you have to become totally convinced that proofreading matters. Even if it doesn't matter to you, it matters to other people. They won't notice if you do proofread but they'll sure notice if you don't. If you're not already one, become a proofreading convert.
- Second, you have to accept this statement as ultimate truth: *There are errors in your paper.* Everybody has them; you do too. These can range from typos (which is the same as an error to anyone reading it) to leaving out words to grammatical mistakes. Expect trouble.
- Third, you have to do it religiously. Get in the habit of proofreading anything you write—even when you sign your name. When you're giving

someone else a paper to read, proofread it at least two or three times. *Slow down.* The slower you go, the more errors you'll see. Look for trouble.

- Fourth, finish your paper in time to put it aside for a day or so or at least a few hours. When you return to the paper, you will see errors you overlooked earlier.

WRITING ON A WORD PROCESSOR

A lot of teachers are like me: Their eyes are tired and they don't want to decipher handwriting day after day, so they require that all outside papers be typed in a professional way. It's true that there are certain times when writing by hand is the better choice, such as when you're working on pieces which require lots of emotion or reflection. Writing turns out differently when you use pen and paper and feel the words in your arm. But anything you write that you want to develop into a full essay will eventually have to be typed. And most of your papers will have to be retyped a time or two to get them right.

One way to cut down on errors caused by rewrite fatigue is to do your writing on a word processor. With a word processor you can move paragraphs around, insert or delete material, catch typos and misspelled words with the spelling checker, and generally save yourself hours of retyping.

Working with a word processor or computer can be frustrating at first, especially the first time you forget to store a document and lose the whole thing after you've been working on it for four hours. But once you learn the basics, you're set. Most colleges now have a computer center for students to use. Not only can you use the machines for free, but you can also get free instruction and help whenever you get into trouble. All you have to do is buy a disk, show up, sit yourself down to a machine, and ask questions. Learn this skill and save your valuable writing time to spend on new creations.

CREDITING YOUR SOURCES

Many of the writing suggestions in the *Expanding the Experience* sections after the exercises ask that you use outside sources such as books, movies, poems, plays, and articles. Getting ideas from other people is natural and a highly prized route to self-education. However, there's a pitfall here—one you may have heard of: *plagiarism.* That's a fancy word for stealing other people's ideas or words without giving them credit for it. Two traps that usually lead to plagiarism are

- writing down words or ideas from a source and forgetting to write down where you got them;

- forgetting that the idea or words have come from someone else; literally thinking they are your own.

There's no need to get yourself into any kind of corner. You don't need to steal other people's ideas. Use whatever you like. The only requirement is that you meticulously acknowledge where the idea or words are from. If you observe the following rules all the time, you should never fall into the plagiarism trap:

- The minute you even look at a book, magazine, newspaper, or other source, write down (on a file card if you like) the *author,* the *title,* the *place of publication,* the *publisher,* and the *date.* For articles or essays, include the *page numbers.*
- If you photocopy any material, write all the information onto the first page immediately and then staple the pages together. Be certain that all the page numbers are legible.
- Later, if you decide to take notes from the source, indicate by the author's last name which source it is, copy your notes carefully, and then be certain to write down the *exact* page number from which you took the note.
- If you take any words directly off the page, *you must put quotation marks around them immediately.* This will remind you that the words are not yours and have to be acknowledged.

The detailed methods of acknowledging your sources are varied and sometimes complicated and certainly beyond the scope of this book. If you write a paper that documents outside sources, you must find a guide that will show you all the subtle distinctions in documentation. The handbook you're using for correctness will usually have instructions for documentation.

Chapter 17

—— FROM FREEWRITE —— TO ESSAY

By the time you reach this chapter, you may have already found ways to turn your freewrites and journal entries from the exercises into shaped papers which you feel good about. But you might also find yourself arriving here with a load of overstuffed parcels, feeling as if you have lots of material but most of it is too soft to mold into anything that will sit upright on a mantelpiece and smile at others.

That's a common feeling—the feeling that "Gee, I have all this stuff pouring out of me and what does it all add up to? What could it possibly mean to anyone else?" At some point, every writer feels that way. But if a piece you've written is meaningful to you, then it has the potential to be meaningful to someone else. And that's true no matter what shape it is in. If you have the desire to turn any piece of writing you've done into a polished essay for others to read, then there's a way to do so. That's what this chapter will help you do.

SHAPING THE MASS

So you have a freewrite in hand—either a short one or a long one. You have two choices and it will not take you more than a minute to decide between them. You can

- ✓ cut it down
- ✓ fatten it up

When you're looking at different pieces of writing and wondering, "What can I make out of these?", your first decision will be either to expand or cut. No matter what the finished product turns out to be, you will begin first with a decision either to expand or cut. This is a crucial decision. It has everything to do with your own concept about the piece. If you have written a three-page journal entry that you want to turn into a 20-line poem, you already see what the first decision is going to be—cut. If, on the other hand, you've spilled out a very emotional one-paragraph writing in an intense response and you absolutely like it and want to make more of it, then clearly your decision here is going to be to expand it. Now, then, how do you go about making these decisions? Suppose you've decided to cut.

Making Cuts

Sometimes when I ask students questions about certain passages, they get flustered and decide on the spot to just draw an X through it and chop it out. Don't do that! Before you cut any hunk out of a piece of writing, be very clear about your *motive* for cutting. Are you cutting it because it embarrasses you?—doesn't have pretty words in it?—doesn't make any sense? Those kinds of emotional cues are reasons *not* to cut. If a section causes you a high negative emotional response, chances are there are some important nuggets buried under that pile. Do not cut that passage. On the contrary, dig into it, perhaps do another freewrite just on that particular passage, and keep asking what it's trying to do. If you listen to what it replies, chances are you will end up expanding that very passage.

Two legitimate cuts would be

- a passage that takes a left-turn when you're riding straight. You're driving smoothly along with your eyes on the road, feeling level, and zap! The car starts tugging left. You can almost *feel* it in your wrist. That's a good prospect for a cut. And if you can't feel it for certain, read your piece to a friend and get a second opinion.

- a passage that is repetitious or overstated. These you can usually spot right off the page in a flash. You've used the same idea but put it in different words. Or you've even used some of the exact words. Or maybe you just kept talking too long. You shouldn't have any trouble making cuts once you recognize a repetition that sounds like bang bang bang bang one too many times.

Making Expansions

The number of times you'll be expanding will outnumber those times you cut three-to-one. I'd estimate that at least 80 percent of the papers I see need *more* rather than less. That means that four out of five of all your papers will need to be expanded rather than cut. Most student writers don't go far enough. They stop too soon. And especially if you're writing rapidly, trying to get a lot of material down, you might give a quick sketch in places where you have lots more information that would add color and detail. Your primary task in expanding your pieces will be to search continuously for such spots and expand on the material. Here are three good candidates for expansions:

- Expand in any place where there is simply not enough information. Your reader can't put the pieces together because some essential ones are missing. This problem is common. Often we know something so well that we forget that others don't have all the information we do. How do you discover these places for yourself? Put yourself in your reader's shoes. Pull back from the material. Keep asking yourself, if I were reading this

194 *From Freewrite to Essay*

for the first time would it be enough? Would it keep me reading? Don't expect your readers to fill in the blanks—even if they could.

- Expand in any spot that begs for more. You can almost feel it as you pass by it. It pulls at you to stop. You want to hover around it. Something's not quite captured. Sometimes you might even feel bored or turned off at these places, but they keep bothering you. Most of these spots you can recognize by continuing to ask yourself as you read over them, "What is missing from my own vision here? What have I left out that was behind the scenes?" Many times you might have to stop right then and there, return to an exercise process, and retrieve a missing piece. But in minutes you've expanded and strengthened your paper with substance instead of hauling words out of a thesaurus.

- Expand in any place in your essay where you want to add more complexity—in other words, more *meaning*. It often happens that meaning arrives with the piece organically and that's always a great gift. Sometimes, however, you have to stop and search for the meaning from scratch because it hasn't yet arrived. But a vital part of any revision is adding meaning. A great part of the richness of writing is to discover meaning for ourselves as we write and then to illuminate that meaning for others. Just as we all like to be told stories, we all like to be told something that has meaning—*inner significance*. "What does this mean?", we think. "Why am I reading this?", your reader will ask. And you are the only one who can answer those questions.

A LOOK AT THREE DRAFTS

Reprinted on the next page is Bean Picking, the prologue to this book. Bean Picking started out as a freewrite dashed off in ten minutes at the end of a hard day of working in a garden. I put it away and forgot about it until I ran across it three years later and decided to rewrite it as the prologue for this book. If you look at the shape it took from freewrite to published piece, you might get some ideas for shaping your own freewrites into essays.

Prologue:
Bean Picking
Published Version

You go out to the garden with a basket on your arm. Three people want beans for dinner. At first the pickings are so slim that you think you'll have to run out and buy beans or maybe just have carrots instead.

With each bean you pick, you think that this is the last one—there don't seem to be any others. Yet you keep finding another bean and then another. You're so busy looking and picking that you don't even notice the bottom of the basket, which is already covered with the long green pods.

When no more beans are in sight, you get down on your knees and search under the bushes. At first your eyes can't pick out the green beans nestled into the green leaves. But you stay with it. Soon your eyes grow accustomed to what they are looking for and you begin to find hidden treasures—many beans in clusters, others resting on the ground waiting for you.

Even so, moments come when you feel impatient with these tiny creatures playing hide-and-seek with you. Moments come when you feel that you're not going fast enough. There are many other things back in the house that need your attention. Picking these beans is interfering with your life.

But the beans don't understand that. They want to wait where they have ripened for your table until you can find them. They've done their job. Now they want you to do yours. So you keep picking. Some of them are not ripe yet. Others have decayed and have to be discarded. Some are so tiny that you think you should throw them away. But you need beans, so you toss them into your basket.

Finally, you've done all you can. You rise, look up at the sky, listen to the birds, take in the canvas of leaves above you, and breathe deeply. The hard part is over. You see that the basket overflows. Each little bean that you harvested has helped to fill it, and now there will be beans for three tonight at dinner. You make your way back to the kitchen, humming a little tune. Something in you remembers that this is how it always is. Yes, bean by bean—that's how everything gets done.

Bean Hunting

Original Freewrite

This morning as I was picking beans, I noticed how harvesting a garden is a lot like writing. The pickings were slim and the kitchen wanted a third of a bin for lunch and I was having a hard time finding enough ripe ones. As I hunted for the beans I heard me talking to myself about the book. I thought, see how little by little each tiny bean adds up and the bin begins to look like it has beans in it? At first you could see the entire bin, but gradually the bottom was covered and before long several layers piled up. Is this the way I can write my book?

I would think there weren't any more beans because I had picked the obvious ones. Then I'd lift the bushes and search and, sure enough, other little treasures were hidden, some resting on the ground, others in purple clusters. Perseverance. Perseverance. That's all it takes, I kept chanting to myself. One motion at a time interlaced with long deep breaths and frequent gazes out to the ocean to return me to myself.

I noticed my impatience in wanting to just get the task done and this impatience would cause me to handle the beans roughly, without appreciation, and at the same time would increase my physical tension. I also at times found myself rejecting certain beans, feeling that they weren't up to snuff, but then realized that they made their own contribution to filling the bin. And isn't my writing just like that? Full of bits and pieces that make a contribution somehow, somewhere? And isn't my impatience with the beans the same impatience I use against myself all the time, especially in writing this book?

Bean by bean, Elaine. That's how your book gets done.

As a writer I still have a certain nostalgia for the truth of the first piece, regardless of whether it's better or worse. But I made a decision and went with it. And that's what you have to do also—make strong decisions about each piece you write and then follow them through. You can easily see the shifts I made in this piece once I decided to move it from a freewrite into a short essay. Had I decided to turn Bean Picking into a poem or a magazine article, the piece would have turned out entirely different in form. But I decided to use it as a prologue to a book about writing and this decision affected the tone, the length, and the content.

The first decision I made was to shift the pronoun "I" to "you" in order to make the experience more universal. This shift doesn't always work; using "you" can be tricky. In this case, I felt using "you" worked and added a better tone to the piece.

The second decision I made was to unpack the first paragraph because it was too dense and moved too fast. In the first freewrite, I told the whole story in the opening paragraph. I needed to loosen it up, slow down the pace, develop the ideas with more details. This first paragraph is a good example of the kind of place that often needs expansion.

I made the opening more dramatic by putting the reader immediately into the scene—a garden. I decided to save the major idea—that the process of bean picking is the same process as writing a book—until the end. I also decided to expand that idea further and make the process of picking beans the same process by which anything else gets done.

I expanded the process of picking the beans with more details and also expanded the concluding paragraph so that it would end with more meaning. I deliberately added *meaning* to the piece.

I omitted the reference to looking at the ocean so as not to confuse the reader. To stop and explain that the garden was near the ocean would have been an unnecessary detour that would have stopped the flow of the essay. The "one motion at a time interlaced with long deep breaths and frequent gazes out to the ocean" was an image I wanted to keep, but chose to cut for the sake of unity. This happens often in writing—you like it but you see it needs to go.

The major shift I made was in tone and voice. I abandoned the interior talking-to-myself voice and took on a strong telling voice. I made up a character—a "you"—and a story.

Most of my editing was substituting poetic words and phrases for ones I felt were ineffective; for example "pickings were slim" and "weren't up to snuff"—both cliches. I added strong sensory images wherever possible.

I changed the title slightly from "hunting" to "picking" because picking was more accurate—the beans were first hunted but then they were picked. Also "hunting" had the connotation of stalking animals in the woods; "picking" sounded folksy, like a down-on-the-farm family.

If you study the two versions side by side, you'll probably discover for yourself most of the ingredients of the revising and editing process.

However, just in case you think there was only a first and second draft (only two drafts almost *never* happens), I'm including also the first revision I made when converting the piece from freewrite to essay—one of four before it became the final form. Without too much explanation, I think you'll see the expansion of areas, while I was working for meaning, and then the paring down again to maintain tone. You'll also see some moving around of details for better placement. This draft represents a common stage in the writing process—the stage where you open up the piece all the way, put in everything important that got left out, and then cut it all back down again to retain unity and tone.

Bean Picking
Second Draft

You go out to the garden with a basket on your arm. Three people want beans for dinner. At first the pickings are so slim that you think you'll have to run out and buy some or maybe just have carrots instead. But you stay in the heat for awhile and keep looking for the little green pods.

You don't notice at first that, as you concentrate on finding the beans, the bottom of the basket is now covered. You keep thinking with every bean you pick that this is the last bean—there don't seem to be any others as you look around.

Then you get down on your knees and lift the bushes and search. At first your eyes can't pick out the green beans nestled into the green leaves. But you keep at it. Soon your eyes grow accustomed to what it is they are looking for and you begin to find hidden treasures—many beans in clusters, others resting on the ground waiting for you.

You pause, look up at the sky, listen to the birds, take in the canvas of leaves above you and you take a deep breath. Something in you has relaxed. You think now you might have enough beans for three people.

Even so, as you continue to pick, moments come when you feel impatient with these tiny creatures playing hide-and-seek with you.

Moments come when you feel impatient with yourself that you're not going fast enough. There are many other things back in the house that need your attention. You want to hurry up and get this over with. Picking these beans is interfering with your life.

But the beans don't understand that. They want to wait where they have ripened for your table until you can find them. They've done their job. Now they wait for you to do yours. You find some others to pick and then discover to your disappointment that they are not yet ripe. You pick others and reject them because they have decayed. Some tiny ones that you pick you think you should throw away. Yet something tells you that they will contribute somehow to filling the basket, so you put them in.

And then an idea comes to you: Harvesting is a lot like writing. You look at the basket and notice that it's filled. You know that each little bean has helped in its own way to complete the harvest. Now there will be beans for three tonight for dinner. You have made it happen with your harvest. You know now that this is the way it is. Bean-by-bean, that's how everything—even your writing—gets done.

Deliberate practice in taking your freewritings and turning them into polished pieces is a direct route to gaining control over your writing—and to discovering your power as a writer. The more you work with the material that comes from you, the more you will see how much of you there is to share with others through your writing.

And now here are some steps to help you with the process.

STEPS FOR TURNING A FREEWRITE INTO AN ESSAY

- Let the freewrite rest for awhile—an hour, a day, a week, a few months. When you take it out, read it through silently. Make corrections. Make notes where you think additions will be needed. Most freewrites will need expanding rather than cutting, at least in the initial stage.

- Read it aloud. Listen for the gaps—gaps in details and information, as well as gaps in meaning. Concentrate at this point on adding meaning, or making your meaning clear. Ask yourself questions about meaning: "Is my deeper, underlying meaning clear? If not, which words or sentences would illuminate this meaning here?" Write notes in the margins about what you want to add. At the top of the freewrite, add a statement: "The real meaning of this freewrite for me is. . . ." Keep that statement in front of you; it is the main idea you want to impart to your reader.

- Read your freewrite over again silently. Look at the structure. Indicate where paragraphs should go; draw arrows to indicate where you might want to transpose material. If you have parts that seem to be interruptions, indicate them. If there are parts of the freewrite that go off in a different direction, consider deleting them. However, you might first freewrite further on these parts to see if you can uncover a better connection. If you do, they could then become part of your essay.

- Write a first full draft, adding the missing parts. As you write more material, work to include vivid details—sensory descriptions, personal observations, anecdotes, specific examples. You might add more material than you will actually end up keeping, but don't inhibit yourself. Don't be afraid to waste words. Give all your ideas and impulses a chance.

- Now consciously let your imagination have a say. Ask yourself: "What could I add that would excite my reader's imagination?" Listen for ideas. Add them if they seem appropriate. This is the stage where you might discover new depths to your freewrite. Stay open to inspiration as you write your first full draft.

- After you complete a full draft which seems to be about the length you want, read it aloud again and this time listen to the rhythms of your sentences. This is the stage at which you should edit your sentences to make them musical. This is also the stage at which you should work on voice. Make adjustments until the voice is strong and sounds like a real person speaking.
- Next, read your full draft aloud to a friend. Let your listener ask questions and point out gaps where more information is needed. Ask your listener also to indicate spots that drag. Make notes and incorporate ideas and suggestions that you like.
- Write another draft . . . and another . . . and another. Now is the time to work layer by layer, looking closely at the sequence of ideas and the general shape the essay is taking. With each successive draft, work for more texture (depth of meaning, sensory details which give images) and a consistent voice. Read each draft aloud and make adjustments until you achieve a strong and unifying voice and tone.
- In your final edit, focus on your introduction and conclusion to be sure that you have taken your reader firmly by the hand, both entering and exiting. The opening and closing should frame your essay, make it more engaging, and also give emphasis to the central meaning of the piece.
- Finally, give your essay a title which illuminates clearly what the piece is about. Don't forget: You can use your title to give additional meaning to what you've written.

Chapter 18

GOING ON

We've reached the last chapter and it's about going on—*you* going on. I'll still be snuggled into these pages waiting for someone else to come along. But you will go on from here and wave to me from your mountaintop. Then you'll keep on going on . . . writing everywhere you go.

Expect to keep writing. Don't quit. Now that you've tapped into your inner self, give yourself a chance to walk out and tell people some things you've discovered. Now that you have acquired the techniques of retrieving important information through meditation, you can use these techniques for any type of writing. No matter what you have to write, remember that you now have the ability to recall genuine, powerful, original material that you can use on the spot.

Keep doing the exercises. Do your favorites over and over. Each time you repeat an exercise, you'll get new material or the same material from different angles. If you discover one particular theme showing up over and over in different exercises, you might decide to follow it through in depth.

Have some fun with the exercises. You might:

✓ Randomly choose a title from one group and a title from another and use them creatively. For example, you could take "A Nightmare" and couple it with "An Eating Experience" to write an imaginative piece. Or you might combine "Today's News" and "Empty Stage" and come up with an unusual idea.

✓ Take different characters from different exercises, put them together, and cook up a plot for them—for example, take one of the characters from "You Are the Camera" and one from "Outrageous Acts" and see what happens.

✓ Write a "mood" autobiography of yourself by putting together a number of the short, personal responses you've written in various exercises.

✓ Choose a particular theme or a particular experience and put it through several related exercises to develop different aspects of it. For example, if romantic relationships have gone sour for you a number of times, you might write about this experience in different ways by putting it through several exercises, such as "First Love," "The Angry Exercise," "Early Rejection," and "Whisper."

✓ Choose a general topic or issue and pick an exercise from different categories to develop many aspects of the topic. For example, you could take the idea of the value of ethnic diversity and write about it in several unrelated exercises such as "Home," "People Watching," "The Other," and "A Modern Hero."

✓ A good way to force yourself to experiment with all the exercises is to put the title of each exercise on a separate slip of paper, put each slip into its own envelope, seal the envelopes, and then choose one each week to do on your own at home. Do this in addition to class work and assignments. Repeating the exercises will yield new material each time. You can also use this same method as a way to put the exercises together in unusual ways.

✓ Interchange parts of different exercises. Do the first three steps of one exercise and the last steps of another exercise and try to make meaning out of it. For example, do steps one to three of "Repeat Performance" and then switch to steps five to eight of "Your Life in Song." Having to put unrelated events together keeps your mind flexible and forces your imagination into service.

✓ Make up your own exercises. All you have to do to make up an exercise is to pay close attention to your life and thoughts. You'll get ideas every day if you look for them. To start, get together with a few friends and talk about ideas you have that would make good exercises.

In the appendix you will find several sample papers that grew out of the exercises. Read these for ideas or use them when you feel stuck; but don't make too much of them or try to copy from them. They are not meant to be examples of how you should write. They are simply a random sample of different ways other writers have used the exercises.

So now I'm going to bow out of here with two final orders.

First, *read.* It's that simple. Next to writing regularly, reading is more important to your development as a writer than anything else I can recommend. Read the great writers, the great thinkers. A special way to read as a writer is to read with a purpose before going to sleep at night. Choose a particular writer who can teach you what you want to learn that week—say Woody Allen to get some wild humor and outlandish actions into your writing; Grace Paley for quirky voice; Loren Eiseley for turning on your sense of wonder; Delmore Schwartz for using dreams as story material; Gurdjieff for shaking up your ideas about reality; Ray Bradbury for transforming the real into the fantastic; Annie Dillard for seeing the world anew; William Faulkner for voluptuous prose; Eudora Welty for creating place. Read some of the best poets— Edna St. Vincent Millay, T. S. Eliot, Adrienne Rich, Garcia Lorca—for planting magnificent sentences in your head. Don't read only to put yourself to sleep. Ease into a state of relaxed attention and then read with the purpose of re-seeding your own writer's garden while you sleep and dream.

I have always liked books that end with a list of other books, and that's exactly what you'll find at the end of this one. The first is a listing of all the books, stories, songs, movies, and poems that have been mentioned or quoted from throughout this book. The second is a short list of books which might prove valuable to you as a writer. And, of course, all of these sources will lead you to other sources, and then to others . . . enough to keep you reading forever.

So now we've really come to the end of this particular journey and the last word I want to leave you with before we say goodbye is this: *Always cut down everything you write into manageable pieces.* Write long, long essays, books, stories, plays, poems—of course. But think about them in small slices. Rather than fighting with huge ideas, fall in love with little pieces of writing, one piece at a time: a four-line description, a six-sentence paragraph, one scene, one moment, a tiny image. Just throw your perfect self out the window and keep writing a little of this and a little of that—things you've been waiting to write. Then watch those pieces pile up into something that eventually will make even you smile. Bit by bit. Bean by bean. Yes indeed. That *is* the way everything gets done.

APPENDIX

A List of Books
Sample Writings
Alphabetical List of Exercises

A LIST OF BOOKS

Sources Mentioned or Quoted in Text

Following is an alphabetical list of sources either mentioned or quoted in this book. Complete publishing data is given so you can locate the sources you are most interested in.

The original date of publication of a piece, if different from the publication of a particular edition, is given immediately after the title. In brackets at the end of entries quoted from in the text of *Writing from the Inner Self*, you will find a page number. This page number indicates the exact page on which you can find the quotation in the edition listed.

Agee, James. *Let Us Now Praise Famous Men*. Boston: Houghton, 1941. [132–33]

American Heritage Dictionary of the English Language. 3rd Edition. New York: Houghton, 1992.

Aurelius, Marcus [A.D. 121–180]. *Meditations*. 1635. Translator, Maxwell Staniforth. New York: Penguin, 1964. [Book X #27, 159]

Bachelard, Gaston. *The Psychoanalysis of Fire*. Boston: Beacon Press, 1964. [1]

Bancroft, Anne. *Zen: Direct Pointing to Reality*. New York: Thames and Hudson, 1991.

Berger, John, et al. *Ways of Seeing*. New York: Viking, 1973. [7; 9]

Bertherat, Therese and Carol Bernstein. *The Body Has Its Reasons*. New York: Avon, 1977. [9]

Bly, Robert. *A Little Book on the Human Shadow*. New York: Harper, 1988. [7]

Bosnak, Robert. *A Little Course in Dreams*. Boston: Shambala, 1988. [17]

Bradbury, Ray. *Dandelion Wine*. 1957. New York: Knopf, 1978. [viii; xiv]

Brodkey, Harold. "First Love and Other Sorrows." 1958. *First Love and Other Sorrows*. New York: Random, 1988.

Brooks, Charles. *Sensory Awareness.* Great Neck, New York: Felix Morrow, 1986.

Browning, Robert. "Soliloquy of the Spanish Cloister." 1842. *The Poetical Works of Robert Browning.* Boston: Houghton, 1974.

Campbell, Joseph. *The Hero with a Thousand Faces.* New Jersey: Princeton, 1949. [391]

Chopra, Deepak. *Quantum Healing.* New York: Bantam, 1989.

Conrad, Joseph. "The Secret Sharer." 1909. *The Portable Conrad.* New York: Penguin, 1976.

Coxhead, David and Susan Hiller. *Dreams: Visions of the Night.* New York: Thames and Hudson, 1976.

The CQ Researcher. [Formerly *Editorial Research Reports*]. Congressional Quarterly Inc., in conjunction with EBSCO Publishing. Washington, D.C.

Crane, Stephen. *The Red Badge of Courage.* 1895. New York: W. W. Norton, 1976.

Debussy, Claude. "La Mer." 1906. Philharmonia Orchestra conducted by Carlo Giulini. Angel Records, 1962.

Dictionary of the History of Ideas. Editor, Philip P. Wiener. New York: Scribners, 1974. 5 vols.

Dillard, Annie. *An American Childhood.* New York: Harper, 1987. [183]

Eco, Umberto and G. B. Zorzoli. *The Picture History of Inventions.* New York: Macmillan, 1961.

Euripides. *The Medea.* 431 B.C. Translated by Rex Warner. *Euripides I.* Chicago: University of Chicago Press, 1955.

"Every Breath You Take." Sting [Gordon Sumner]. The Police. *Synchronicity.* A&M Records, 1983.

"Far Away Places." 1948. Joan Witney and Alex Kramer. Willie Nelson/Leon Russell. *One for the Road.* Columbia Records, 1980.

Fitzgerald, F. Scott. "Babylon Revisited." 1931. *The Stories of F. Scott Fitzgerald.* New York: Scribner's, 1951. [390]

Forster, E. M. *Aspects of the Novel.* 1927. New York: Harcourt, 1955. [28; 47]

———. *Howards End.* 1921. New York: Random, 1989. [86]

Franck, Frederick. *The Zen of Seeing.* Random, 1973. [xx; 15; xi]

Freud, Sigmund. *The Interpretation of Dreams.* 1900. New York: Avon, 1965.

Frost, Robert. 1916. "The Road Not Taken." *A Selection of Robert Frost's Poems.* New York: Holt, 1971.

Gallwey, Timothy W. *The Inner Game of Tennis.* New York: Bantam, 1974. [9]

Gray, Henry. *Gray's Anatomy.* 1858. Philadelphia: Running Press, 1974.

Gurdjieff. *Views from the Real World.* New York: Dutton, 1973. [281]

Halpern, Daniel. *Plays in One Act.* Hopewell, N.J.: Echo, 1991.

Humphrey, Robert. *Stream of Consciousness in the Modern Novel.* Berkeley: University of California Press, 1954.

"Jalousie." 1926. Jacob Gade and Vera Bloom. Frankie Laine. *16 Most Requested Songs.* Legacy Records, 1959.

James, William. *The Principles of Psychology.* 1890. New York: Dover, 1950.

King, Martin Luther, Jr. "Letter from the Birmingham City Jail." 1963. *The Essential Writings of Martin Luther King.* San Francisco: Harper, 1986.

Knowles, John. *A Separate Peace.* 1960. New York: Bantam, 1972. [44]

Leboyer, Frederick. *Birth without Violence.* New York: Knopf, 1975.

Lockhart, Russell. *Words as Eggs.* Dallas: Spring, 1983. [100]

Lowen, Alexander. *Fear of Life.* New York: Macmillan, 1980. [187]

Manguel, Alberto and Gianni Guadalupi. *The Dictionary of Imaginary Places.* New York: Macmillan, 1980.

Maugham, W. Somerset. "An Appointment in Samarra." From *Sheppey.* 1933. *The Collected Plays,* vol. III. London: Heinemann, 1955. [298]

May, Rollo. *The Courage to Create*. New York: Norton, 1975.

Miller, Casey and Kate Swift. *The Handbook of Nonsexist Writing*. New York: Harper, 1988. [139]

Miller, Jim, ed. *The Rolling Stone Illustrated History of Rock and Roll*. New York: Random, 1976.

Mitford, Nancy. *The Pursuit of Love*. New York: Random, 1945. [3]

Oxford English Dictionary (OED). 1933. Oxford, England: Clarendon, 1961. 11 vols.

Paine, Thomas. "Common Sense." 1776. *Basic Writings of Thomas Paine*. New York: Willey, 1942.

Pareles, Jon and Patricia Romanowski, eds. *The Rolling Stone Encyclopedia of Rock and Roll*. New York: Rolling Stone Press, 1983.

Pirsig, Robert. *Zen and the Art of Motorcycle Maintenance*. New York: Bantam, 1974. [267]

Proust, Marcel. *Swann's Way*. New York: Random, 1928. [611]

Rashomon. Director and writer, Akira Kurosawa. 1950. With Toshiro Mifune. Embassy VHS, 1986. 83 min.

Repeat Performance. Director, Alfred Werker. Writer, Walter Bullock. With Louis Hayward and Joan Leslie. Eagle/Lion, 1947. 93 min.

Rubin, Theodore Isaac. *The Angry Book*. New York: Macmillan, 1969.

Saint-Exupéry, Antoine de. *The Little Prince*. 1943. New York: Harcourt, 1971. [9]

Shakespeare, William. *Hamlet*. 1622. New York: New American, 1987. [II.ii. 253–54]

——. *Othello*. 1622. New Haven: Yale University, 1947.

Sondheim, Stephen. "Finishing the Hat." *Sunday in the Park with George*. RCA, Original Cast Recording, 1984.

State of the World: A Worldwatch Institute Report on Progress Toward a Sustainable Society. Editor, Lester Brown. New York: Norton, 1991.

Strich, Christian. *Fellini's Faces: 418 Photographs from the Archives of Federico Fellini.* New York: Holt, 1981.

Suzuki, Shuryu. *Zen Mind, Beginner's Mind.* New York: Weatherhill, 1970.

Switch. Director and writer, Blake Edwards. With Ellen Barkin. HBO video, 1991. 104 minutes.

Takahashi, Shinkichi. "Potato." Translator, Harold Wright. *Leaping Poetry.* Editor, Robert Bly. Boston: Beacon, 1975. [19]

Tavris, Carol. *Anger: The Misunderstood Emotion.* New York: Simon and Schuster, 1982.

Thoreau, Henry David. "Civil Disobedience." 1849 ["Resistance to Civil Government"]. *Walden and Civil Disobedience.* New York: Penguin, 1983.

"Too Young." 1951. Sid Lippman and Sylvia Dee. Nat King Cole. *Unforgettable.* Capitol Records, 1989. (See also: Natalie Cole. *Unforgettable.* Elektra, 1991.)

Turgenev, Ivan. "First Love." *First Love and Other Stories.* New York: Scribners, 1904.

Verny, Thomas. *The Secret Life of the Unborn Child.* New York: Summit Books, 1981.

Welty, Eudora. *The Eye of the Story.* Random, 1979. [354]

————. "Livvie." 1943. *Selected Stories of Eudora Welty.* New York: Random, 1971. [154b]

Wilder, Alec. *American Popular Song.* New York: Oxford, 1972.

A Few Books on Writing

Appelbaum, Judith. *How to Get Happily Published.* 1988. New York: Harper, 1992.

Bradbury, Ray. *Zen in the Art of Writing.* Santa Barbara: CAPRA Press, 1990.

Brande, Dorothea. *Becoming a Writer.* 1934. Los Angeles: J. P. Tarcher, 1981.

Dillard, Annie. *The Writing Life.* New York: Harper & Row, 1989.

Elbow, Peter. *Writing without Teachers*. New York: Oxford University Press, 1973.

Garrison, Roger. *How a Writer Works*. New York: Harper & Row, 1981.

Goldberg, Natalie. *Writing Down the Bones*. Boston: Shambhala Publications, 1986.

Rico, Gabriele Lusser. *Writing the Natural Way*. Los Angeles: Tarcher, 1983.

Silverman, Jay, Elaine Hughes, Diana Roberts Wienbroer. *Rules of Thumb: A Guide for Writers*. New York: McGraw, 1993.

Ueland, Brenda. *If You Want to Write*. 1938. St. Paul: Graywolf Press, 1987.

SAMPLE WRITINGS

The sample writings are just that—some samples of how other writers have responded to the exercises. At the bottom of each page, you will find the name of the exercise that inspired the writing. Most of the papers were written in class as journal entries and later some of them were revised into short papers. They are not put here as models for you to imitate but as idea sparkers when you need them. Use them sparingly: Let your own experiences lead your writing.

A Sleigh Ride by Karla Fitzgerald

A Day at the Beach by John Falino

That Winning Season by Robert N. Bruck

The Cow's Head by Darren Barje

Voice in My Head by Robin Simkins

The Fort by Cynthia Davis

Summer Reading by Joe Dourigan

The Joys of Immaturity by Gregory J. Garry

Remembering Stevie Ray Vaughan by Robert Echeverria

Kiss Me . . . I'm Irresistible by Gregory Schweizer

Ethel by Emilie Borg

The Hungry of America: People Nobody Wants to Help by Andrew Cohen

A Sleigh Ride

by Karla Fitzgerald

It is wintertime and the leaves are gone from the trees. Fresh snow is piling up on the older snow. When I look down the street and see the snow sparkling on the empty branches I get a peaceful feeling. My family and I are outside in the snow. I can see the mist forming as our breath meets the cold air.

In front of the house my sisters frolic in the snow. My mother is wearing a long red winter coat and black boots but she still appears to be cold. In her hands is a shiny silver shovel. She is removing snow from the driveway. She has formed a snow mountain with the snow that has been removed.

Our dog, Toni, is also outside with us. Toni is a black Standard Poodle. She is sliding on the sidewalk on the thin, smooth sheet of ice that has formed. I see her mouth slightly open and her white teeth are showing. A mist appears as her breath hits the air.

My father is approaching Toni. Around her neck he places a long white string. I follow the string to see what is attached to it. The object appears to be long and not very high off the ground. There are red pieces of metal that touch the ground under long strips of wood.

I am being picked up and placed on the light brown strips of wood. The two big hands remain wrapped around me to help support my back so that I sit up straight. Suddenly I begin to get nervous. I am unsure of what will happen. My hands become sweaty inside my mittens. My pink snowsuit with Winnie-the-Pooh embroidered on it also begins to feel too warm.

My father's voice sounds but I do not understand what he says. Suddenly I find myself in motion. The object on which I am seated is gliding across the snow and ice. In front of me Toni seems to be running at top speed. Objects around me appear to be flying by. I open my mouth to call for help but hear no sound. I can still feel the two big hands that offer me support wrapped around me. I am scared and wish to stop.

Finally I am lifted off the speeding object and I am in my father's arms. Two cold rivers run down my cheeks. My eyes are blurry and my eyelashes become stiff. A feeling of security comes from the two arms holding me. I hope that I will not have to endure such an ordeal again.

A Day at the Beach
by John Falino

Water is one of the four elements necessary for our survival on the planet. We could not live one day without water. Water, which is referred to by scientists as H_2O, is often looked at as a very peaceful thing of nature, and many people often take pleasure in drinking it. But the peacefulness that water presents can often be deceiving. People often have the tendency to overlook the power of water and, because of this, they become the victims of tragic accidents and drownings.

When I was about ten years old, my entire family went to the beach for the day. When we arrived, the first thing I saw was the Atlantic Ocean. It looked so big and peaceful that I could hardly wait to jump right in. As I ran towards the shore, I could see the waves breaking towards me, and the wind the ocean created felt cool on my body. When I reached the edge of the water, I could feel that the water was cold, and "goose bumps" started to spread throughout my entire body. Without thinking, I then sprinted into the water, trying to avoid the coldness of the water. Once I was in, I started swimming and splashing and was having the greatest time. I could hear my mother yelling to me, "Don't go too far out or else the undertow will pull you out and you will not be able to get back in." I thought to myself, she's crazy, the water cannot hurt me.

After about an hour of swimming, I started to get really confident in the water, and I thought I was in complete control. I gradually started to go further and further out, and before I knew it, the water was over my head. For some reason, I immediately panicked and started trying to make my way back to shore. It seemed that the faster I swam, the slower I would move. My heart started beating really fast and I became real tired. My head then started to go under and I was swallowing water. At that point, I blacked out.

The next thing I remember is lying on the beach and looking up and seeing about a hundred people looking down at me. What had apparently happened is one of the lifeguards noticed that I was drowning and blew the whistle. They all came out and rescued me and brought me onto shore. They pumped the water out of me through my mouth and that was when I woke up. Although I had been so close to dying, I did not have to go to the hospital, so I just went home with my parents that day. I am very grateful to the lifeguards who rescued me and I feel I owe them my life.

Until that memorable experience I had in the ocean, I always thought that water was harmless and peaceful. I now know not to take water for granted because it can sneak up and get you when you least expect it. Although the ocean almost took my life from me, I still go swimming and participate in several water activities. I feel that I have once again become real comfortable in the water, but I now know that, as friendly as the water looks, it can turn into your enemy at any given time.

That Winning Season

by Robert N. Bruck

In the fall of 1983, I was appointed captain of the high school soccer team. My responsibilities included leading the warm-up drills, going out for the coin toss before each game, and most importantly carrying the soccer balls to practice! I was eagerly anticipating the chance to lead our team to a successful season, as I had inherited a team that had won only one out of eleven games the previous year.

By late September our team was well into the third week of practices and only fourteen young men had joined the squad. It takes eleven players to have an official team, but on most other clubs, there are close to twenty players. The reason for the extra players is because of the expectation of injuries and absences during the season. The fact that only fourteen players turned out for the "Falcons" clearly demonstrated the lack of spirit and enthusiasm that existed for our team and in the school. Nevertheless, five days a week at three in the afternoon our team would meet at a park to practice and fine tune our skills.

Our coach always arrived at the field at three o'clock, promptly. If any teammate arrived one minute late for practice, the coach would discharge that person and make him do a specific chore in school. One of the chores included scraping the bottom of the school desks—a most disgusting task, as any high school student is aware of the hazardous wastes deposited under desks. Other duties included washing out the water fountains in the gym and dusting "Coach" magazines in the library.

Coach did in fact become the only force that united this ill-spirited group of high school teens. He was five feet eight inches tall, weighed approximately two hundred fifty pounds, was well over fifty, a former army drill sergeant, and a bachelor who lived with his mother. Everyone on the team silently respected him merely as a coach, but he tried to give us the impression that, if he'd desired to, he could have become a doctor. Of course, it had been his choice and he "C H O S E" to be a physical education teacher.

Coach did unite us as a team but not in the way that most people would think a coach should. I felt that because all fourteen players literally despised him, it gave us a special energy out on the field. During tough, cold autumn practice sessions, we used to grin and bite our lips just thinking of how much we all hated him.

During practices, as well as in official games, if a player made a mistake on the field, Coach would embarrass us to no end. He would fly off the bench, and with a deep breath start screaming, "You f---ing panty waists. Can't you do anything right? Didn't you see that g-d damn play coming? Why don't you use the little brains you got?!" Since we were in a public park, this kind of outburst was obviously extremely embarrassing, especially because there were spectators. He would often torture us at half-time. If he felt we did not give a full effort in the first half he would drain all the water bottles on the grass right in front of us. If one of the players were to curse on the field, the next day Coach would devise another new and exciting chore for us to perform. Coach was also very strict on the uniforms we had to play in. If one of us wore navy blue shorts instead of the traditional black ones, he would not hesitate to bench the player even at the cost of playing with less than eleven men on the field.

The season turned out to be a long and aggravating one as our first goal did not come until the seventh game. Needless to say we had lost the first ten games all by great margins. But we had a large following of spectators from the neighborhood who used to cheer us on and the culmination of that season was our final game in front of a large crowd of mothers, fathers, faculty, and students. As the team was getting dressed for the game there was a slightly different feeling in the atmosphere. Something was different about this game. We were somehow inspired to play our guts out one last time.

Right from the start we played the best game of our lives. Passes were actually being completed. We were diving, hitting, and running like a real team. For the first time we actually played with pride. With only five minutes left in the game, we were winning two goals to none. We were really up emotionally and felt the victory in our grasps. Even our supporters were screaming and cheering with our imminent victory. Then lightning struck. Like the German blitzkrieg of Poland we were overwhelmed by three quick goals. At this point the coach really let himself go. He began yelling with more fervor than ever before. It sounded as if the Concorde jet was landing on the field. Even the spectators were embarrassed for us. The parents and the faculty were shocked.

After such a long and grudging season I could not take it any more. I began yelling back, harder than he ever did, "Why don't you get your fat ass off the sidelines and show us what you want us to do!" Finally, as the finishing touch, I reached down into my jockstrap and pulled out the plastic cup that protected my genitals. I tossed the cup like a frisbee and it landed at his feet.

All this was happening while the game was still being played. As I marched off the field, many of the parents tried to calm me down. The coach continued yelling from the sidelines at my remaining teammates. Then one by one the other seniors began tossing their cups in a virtual rainstorm of flying plastic triangular frisbees as they too walked off the field. It was a shame, but this was the only satisfaction I received out of the whole season—from a sport that I had loved.

The Cow's Head

by Darren Barje

It seems that everyone has a particular drawer in the house where a wide assortment of "junk" can be found. In my house, this drawer is located in the kitchen. In it you can find anything from an egg slicer to a rubber band. The other day, while searching for a paper clip, I came across one of the strangest utensils I have ever seen.

The object is made of a heavy cast iron which makes it cold to the touch. It is circular in shape and is about the size of a hockey puck. The utensil opens on a single hinge into two equal halves. The strangest part is that it has a cow's face on both sides. It was this feature which attracted me to the utensil in the first place.

At first I had absolutely no idea what this thing was until I opened it and found that it had instructions engraved on one of its halves. The exact words read: "Place meat between two pieces of wax paper and press upper part down." That was when I figured out that it was used to make hamburger patties.

The hamburger maker looks really old, as if we'd had it in the house for many years, but I have never seen anyone in the family use it. I had always thought you just mashed the ground meat down with your hands and more or less formed it into the circular hamburger shape. I never knew you could use a contraption such as this to make perfectly round burgers. I don't understand why anyone would take the time to make their hamburgers this way, especially if they were making a lot of them. I think it would be very messy and time consuming to use a utensil like this. Also, judging from its appearance, it must make very thin burgers because it is less than half an inch thick.

The hamburger maker is stamped "Made in Taiwan" but no one in my family knows where it was actually purchased. Since it looks so old I figure maybe it came from a garage sale. The utensil has no complex parts, but, oddly enough, the cow's head is extremely detailed and looks as though it were stenciled by hand.

The utensil is considerably heavy so it may have been fairly expensive to manufacture because of all the metal used in it. The metal on the side of the utensil looks like it was dripping at one point which leads me to believe that the metal used was a liquid which was then poured into a mold and left to cool until it hardened.

The edges of the burger maker are rough and jagged so the manufacturer probably pulled it right out of the mold when it was hard and stuck the two halves together without any further polishing. Aside from the two halves, which snap together on a hinge, there are no removable parts. This is evidence that probably very few steps were taken in the production of the utensil. Since the two halves are identical, the manufacturer didn't even need to use many molds since the same ones could be used over and over.

I had never used this utensil before, so after studying it closely for a long time, I felt as though I had to at least make an attempt at getting the thing to work. I went to the freezer and took out some hamburger meat. After softening it up a bit in the microwave, I proceeded to stick a piece of the meat into the burger maker. I squeezed it closed but I wasn't sure of how long it was supposed to stay in the mold. I figured five minutes was long enough and opened it. To my surprise the thing actually worked. The only problem was that, although the burger was perfectly shaped, it came out very thin and therefore didn't appeal to me. So I didn't eat it . . . I just got into the car and drove over to McDonald's for a Big Mac.

Voice in My Head

by Robin Simkins

Voice in my head—voice in my head? That's hysterical! I'm always here don't you know that? You always talk to me—are you crazy and I know you don't think so. Cool exercise I know you like to write. Too bad you're tired and haven't done your Dr. Ash reflection. Hey she said to relax. You're just too busy need to sleep take a load off. Stop stopping and putting your hand over your face—you know what I say is true. Remember when you were a freshman and you always skipped because it was raining? Yeah Yeah that's old news you talked about that yesterday. Don't usually write like this huh? This is rather up & down for your style. I bet you won't even be able to read it later. Hand tired? Too bad b/c you know I keep on talking talking talking!

Get excited about tonite. It'll be fine. Don't worry—Yeah go ahead & wear your hair down. need a nap. Snuffleupagus nose. You know you wish it would quit running stream of consciousness. Waiting for Godot. You need to write Mr Meeks and thank him for his help and his class. Tom never called back. real nice. Deep breath that's it Don't get too relaxed or you'll never get that reflxn done. Pretty handy abbreviation that "xn" for you isn't it? Man you never write this messy. Chicken scratch. "She can write & draw but she can't cut"—2nd grade Mrs. Mc-Bride Hey I knew that. You knew that. Good thing you're not an art major anymore huh. Always getting Kim in h.s. to cut your mats.

Well I'm going to write neater now. Have more purpose. This looks like 2 different people wrote it. The same main wandering thoughts are going thru my head. I do always talk to myself, usually in my head. When I was little I even noticed it. Asking myself my opinion or whatever. Then other people had imaginary friends so I thought I had to give her/him/whatever a name. I knew people had last names like Green, White, Black, Brown, etc., and my mom liked Barbra Striesand so I named her Barbara Blue. I think that's why I chose Barbra, I don't know. But in my head I spelled it Barbara. I remember telling Merry her name in the living room on Henry Street with the off-white shag carpet. We were by the door on the gold & off-white long curvy sofa—no I was; she was standing up I think. The brown end table by the end of the sofa was by the door and Heidi used to run around the table leg because she was excited about going outside.

The Fort

by Cynthia Davis

The fort was a chaotic configuration of cement slabs at the end of a long sand spit in Watch Hill, Rhode Island. Old mortar shells lay around it, sometimes half buried in the ocean water. It was a good half hour walk from the beach club. We'd take picnics on hot sunny days. It was not just physically removed from us; it was removed by some other eerie, timeless dimension. We always expected to find a skull. We looked and hoped for such a discovery with fear and desire.

Part of the fort was below sea level. You went downstairs into the dark, dank rooms that smelled of urine. There were numerous initials—of both ancient and modern vintage—and a special saying with the word "Charlie" in it which we recognized as having to do with the old war near the beginning of the century. There were long shafts and planks of metal. Were these old planes that had crashed? The fort was only about twenty feet above sea level, with its basement area below sea level. But the ocean never got in when the fort was ours.

We were a gang of kids ages eight to twelve, and seven or so of us would trek out the two and a half mile sand spit separating our world from the fort. There was never adult supervision, but we didn't kiss or chase at the fort. It was too eerie. On those warm sunny days, it had some pact with death. We were always out to find the treasure of a skull. Occasionally a helmet surfaced, enough to keep us going back again and again. Always there were carcasses of bombs and other less recognizable objects. Had they practiced for war here, on the Rhode Island coast?

The spit had once been thickly settled with three-story wooden summer homes. The hurricane of '38 washed them all away, together with a lot of land. I used to look with awe at old pictures of what had once occupied that sandy finger. Scarcely a wooden foundation had survived the storm. Once, very civilized homes had even nestled right up against the old fort. It felt like the hurricane of '38 had happened a very long time ago in my child's view of time.

Our picnics at the fort took place in the early '50s. In 1954 Hurricane Carol swept the ancient, ghostly fort away along with the spit of land we had walked on. The fort was a lost Atlantis when I was a child: a hidden world, elusive to us when we visited it in the sunshine, and yet it was the fresh salt air of our childhood.

Summer Reading

by Joe Dourigan

I'm sitting on my front porch in Vermont and I'm reading *Gulliver's Travels*. It's a book I have to read for the upcoming high school year and I'm not happy about it.

I'm sitting in this rocking chair and I'm looking for any excuse to stop reading. Salvation is a door shot away and comes in the form of the girl-next-door. She is two years younger than I am and she's a knockout.

My eyes follow every move as she slowly makes way to the dock in her very tight black bathing suit. I hear the creaking of the dock as she walks to the edge. I look at my book and hastily throw it into my chair. I get up and quickly shut the noisy screen door and walk to the dock, looking at the water and stretching my body. I'm trying to be inconspicuous and maintain some of my adolescent cool.

She notices me before she jumps in and asks what I am doing up so early. I pause for a second, trying to think of the best answer to impress her with. I lean my bare foot into the water, kick it around a bit, and then casually say, "I'm reading this really interesting book. . . . "

I know by her facial reaction that she's impressed. She says, "Oh I didn't know you were much of a reader, Joe. What are you reading?"

I say with confidence, *"Gulliver's Travels."*

"Oh," she replies, "that's a great book, isn't it? How far have you gotten?"

I had only read the first couple of pages but sometimes the truth can be ugly. So, instead, I say, "Most of the book." She then starts asking me questions at a titillating rate. I am flabbergasted, but, as coolness is my main priority in this encounter, I tell her that I want to read the book over again before I make any total impression.

She jumps into the water and looks back at me and says, "Why don't you come over if you have any questions and we'll talk about it."

I reply nonchalantly, "Okay. Maybe I will."

But inside I am higher than any kite. I turn around and walk back to the house and my book. "Yep," I think to myself. "Reading is definitely a good thing."

The Joys of Immaturity

by Gregory J. Garry

As a child, I was very mistrustful of adults. I saw them as bizarre, staunch, boring and quite nasty on occasion. They watched me with that disapproving eye, recognizing faults rather than attributes. They seemed quite lifeless, almost like statues. Being the youngest in a family of much older children, I was alone much of the time. I had to create an entire universe of my own to amuse myself. My incessant playing, chanting, and talking to myself made my elders afraid of me, so they discouraged this behavior, because they couldn't comprehend it. My early disillusionment with the adult world has carried over into my own "adulthood," and it now encompasses all of society. I still get terribly annoyed with unimaginative people. They bore me terribly.

The narrator's statement in *The Little Prince* simply expresses the fact that, through the eyes of a child, the adult world isn't very impressive. It doesn't seem that adults realize everything going on around them. The reason they couldn't see what the narrator's picture really was illustrates their lack of imagination and perception. Also, in contrast to a child, adults don't seem to be truly happy with their lives. To be an adult means to reach the point where reality dominates over fantasy and your imagination slowly disintegrates. Grown ups have seen the world over, experiencing a myriad of emotions, such as joy and pain, sometimes coming up scarred because of it. They don't have the time, patience, or capacity to really enjoy life. They can't see the entire world the way children can. In a sense, adults reach a kind of stagnation.

Children, on the other hand, view the world with wide eyed wonder and awe, without pretense or prejudice of any kind. Their lack of experience and worldliness causes them to see things most of us cannot, which is their own inborn wisdom. It is very exciting to see a child in amazement at learning something new. Their imaginations are an open door through which they can enter marvelous worlds and do whatever they dream to. Adults see this whimsical behavior as reckless and futile, yet they themselves would be a bit better off if they had an open mind and imaginations of their own. Most children become discouraged by their parents telling them to behave and act in a mature fashion.

While it is good to handle serious situations in an adult, mature manner, why leave all the frivolity out of life by closing your mind? It's like losing your peripheral vision, only seeing ahead, not taking time to savor each moment fully and become aware of the veritable wonderland around you. I often pity the melancholy, over-serious person who never really seems to *live*. I can't really see an accountant, mortician, or a nun letting their hair down and having a wild time, recharging their "batteries."

It is this childlike innocence which helps us deal with adversity in our everyday lives. God knows my "immaturity" has gotten me through some rough periods. I remember a song from my favorite Disney cartoon, *Peter Pan,* that really sums up the theme of the little prince's statement and my theory on life in general. "If growing up means it would be beneath my dignity to climb a tree, then I won't grow up, not me!", declares the anthemic message: If being an adult means compromising the things I enjoy doing, whatever that may be, then the hell with being an adult!

I do what I want to do, even if it's considered immature. I won't let the adults change me into one of them. I intend to maintain an active imagination, keep a sense of humor, and nurture my heart's childlike wonder. Then I will be a well-adjusted grown up with a dazzling life. And that is true maturity.

Remembering Stevie Ray Vaughan
by Robert Echeverria

There are very few people who can understand how much his music means to me. So far, only Linda and Ivan can seem to relate to my feelings.

Everytime I hear "Lenny," I remember the day he died. Walking up the stairs with my mom, I overheard my brother listening to the song. I opened the door to our room and my brother said, "Did you hear? Stevie's dead."

It took awhile to hit, but when it did, it hit hard. I remember sitting down looking at the cover of *Texas Flood* and crying my brains out. I had never cried for anyone this way before—or since. I sort of felt stupid. I even told my brother that I was being stupid for crying like that. But I just continued to cry. I cried all day long. I cried on the way to Doreen's house, on the way to work—I couldn't stop. And I felt so bad.

Why? I kept asking myself. Why? He'd just finished piecing his life together. He had stopped drinking, he was supposed to get married, and his birthday was only a few days away. How can anyone who means so much to the world and makes so many people happy with his music just be taken away like that?

I remembered all the days of my own life that Stevie Ray pulled me through just by his music. He is my inspiration. If I only had the chance to meet him all I would say to him is, "Thank you. Thank you for making life a little easier and happier. Thank you for making me smile every once in awhile."

The way he played, the way he sang, everything about him just fills me with emotion. I get chills, I get the blues. I get a whole orchestra of emotions just from seeing him and listening to him. No one has ever moved me like this before.

Even though he's gone, I still listen to him almost every day. I find myself humming his songs all the time. He's such a big piece of my life and I miss him and, even though I listen to him and watch videos all the time, I know I'll never get tired of him. The older I get, the more reasons I find to like him and I'm grateful to have someone like Stevie Ray to inspire me in my life and in my own music.

Kiss Me . . . I'm Irresistible

by Gregory Schweizer

It was November 5, and coincidentally I had to have 5 contact sheets full of "street people", for a photo essay by 1:30 p.m. on, ha, November 6. There is no time like the last minute. Let me tell you:

It was frigid and the sky was bluest blue; no clouds. The sidewalk was frozen. People pumped up and down the block at a frantic pace. Keeping warm, unlike me. Fingerless gloves fingering a camera that is made of the best conductor of cold since ice. No time like the last minute; that's me.

A greasy, wrinkled dunkin donuts coffee cup was all he had that he wasn't already wearing. Seven pennies, a quarter and a subway token kept it from blowing away. Hair hung all over his face in oily strands. His body started at the top as a head and gradually grew huge as it got closer to the ground; like a mountain. He wasn't the least bit embarrassed or ashamed to pick his nose, no matter who was watching. Even worse, he urinated in the middle of the sidewalk. He looked like Ernest Hemingway . . . sort of. Except bigger and . . . well maybe if Hemingway hadn't really killed himself and he was sitting right in front of me. No. Here was a man with no discretion or brains; why else would he be sitting outside when the rest of the homeless population were crowding the subways and bus terminals keeping warm? (Because he's Ernest Hemingway and *real* men don't sleep in subways where it's warm.) He wasn't Ernest Hemingway, I know. It was just one of those private jokes that I tell myself to keep entertained when I am not really interested in being where I am. His eyes moved independently and in different directions. All I could do is think stupidly of Sammy Davis, Jr., Peter Falk and Sandy Duncan. I couldn't tell if his was a glass eye. "Sleep, you moron, sleep. I'm freezing," kept droning in my head like a mantra everytime my brain hosted another witless thought.

Some more people rilled by, ignoring the fact that I might be trying to get a shot of this guy. Some Wall Street suits looked at both of us through their horn rimmed glasses as if we belonged in the same boat. Morons. Coats wide open, for fashion's sake, trying to catch a cab on the coldest day of the year. You should have seen them: haircuts by Dagwood Bumstead, charcoal suits, brightly colored paisley ties with matching suspenders, iron jaw lines, Italian shoes and probably a shark's sense of sympathy. Maybe they were G-men. Everybody wants to look like Clark Kent these days.

I just looked for a while, thinking. I had forgotten about the cold and just started to sleep standing up, my eyes open and drying out in the wind.

"KISS ME . . . I'M IRRESISTIBLE!!" He rasped in the loudest voice I think his lungs and larynx could've managed. He was suddenly standing. I turned around expecting, or more hoping, to see a lady cop swinging her stick and snapping her gum with a Brooklyn attitude, maybe some woman in tight pants, or just someone presumptuous looking enough to provoke this bum into standing with his arms open, expecting a kiss from somebody. The blood rushed to my face when I realized that the invitation was to me and probably to shame me for not moving on like everyone else. My ears burned and my nose dripped. For a dumbfounded moment I felt almost compelled to take this guy in my arms and kiss him. I didn't. But for just a second, I almost did.

Ethel

by Emilie Borg

Hi, my name is Ethel. I said Ethel. Yes, that's right. Are you sure you want to talk? You're sure? A lot of people say they . . . because if you're. . . . Yes, I live alone, at least for now. My husband Harry died last year. I have a daughter, she wants me to come and live with them but I don't want to.

I miss him, Harry. I come out here every day to this spot and I walk, walk on the beach. It's become a necessity for me. Harry died in the afternoon. I put him in the car and I brought him out here. He was so heavy—you can't imagine. I didn't think I was going to make it, but I did.

I brought him right to this spot, this spot you and I are standing on, and then I dragged him out to the water and put him in. I'm very proud of myself. Yes sir, let me tell you, it wasn't easy. You see, Harry didn't want to go into the earth, to be suffocated by . . . I understand. He had already been suffocated by too many things in his life.

Are you really interested in all this because I don't want to be . . . You sure? You know, I'm lucky. I got away with it. They just wrote me off as some crazy old lady. They didn't understand, wouldn't understand. Won't be able to fight my daughter off for very much longer. She'll be dragging me to their house soon—just like I dragged Harry out here. Well, not exactly. I tell you, I hope to hell I give them as much of a struggle as Harry did me. Who knows what they'll do to me when I die. They won't bring me out here, that's for sure. So now I come out every day and try and get as much air as I can now, while I still can, if you know what I mean. Want to take a walk? You see that. . . .

The Hungry of America:
People Nobody Wants to Help
by Andrew Cohen

More people than you would expect are hungry. Many people think hunger is only a problem in other countries, and not a problem here in America. That thinking is half the problem. The truth is, that America is the only western-civilized country that has a hunger problem (Brown). America clearly has the resources to entirely eliminate hunger. The only thing stopping it seems to be a "lack of commitment" (Segal 2).

Today in America, there are more people hungry and more people living in poverty than ever before. According to Dr. Larry Brown, "low wage jobs, and plant closings" are a big part of the problem. Today more than ever, there are more and more middle class families going hungry. These families don't qualify for any government assistance because in order to receive assistance you can't have more than $6,000 in assets (Citizens' 63). These people are faced with a major decision; whether to get rid of all possessions to get aid, or keep what little they have and receive no aid. If you are lucky enough to receive government assistance, what is given to you isn't nearly enough. For example, food stamps aren't based on what it costs to buy food. They're based on a "desired federal expenditure level, which was set first irrespective of human need" (Citizens' 62). The government clearly doesn't care about people's needs; all they seem to care about is money.

There are many myths concerning the poor and hungry. Among them is the "poor in spirit" theory: Roy Lubove states "people are poor from the unwise use of resources, originating in ignorance, from a wrong set of values" (qtd. in Segal 3). These myths are just another excuse for our government's lack of assistance to the needy.

There are many serious problems the hungry face, besides being hungry. "Hunger affects not only the body but the mind" (Citizens' 54). The feeling of failure runs rampant among many who have lost their jobs. These people feel somehow that it is their fault, like they failed (Grant). Low self-esteem is another wide spread problem among the hungry. Many blame themselves for their problems and troubles. "Sharpest perhaps is the shame felt by parents who cannot provide food for their children" (Citizens' 54). Alcoholism is another problem found around families who are desperate and hungry. These people feel worthless and foresee no help coming in the future; so they turn to the bottle for escape. Adding to the loss of self-esteem is the humiliation of applying for assistance (Citizens' 56). When you apply for assistance, you are asked extensive personal questions about every aspect of your life, all of which contributes to a degrading feeling. Many contemplate suicide as their only way out (Grant). Children suffer greatly both mentally and physically when their parents can no longer provide for them. Fathers leave their families because they simply can't provide for them. "Children become scapegoats for the pain and humiliation of the parents" (Citizens' 56). This all too often leads to child abuse.

Many government policies are preventing families from getting assistance, rather than helping families receive assistance. Hunger isn't present here in America because of lack of food, but rather because of "economic disparities, and bad government policies" (Brown). The belief in trickle-down economics by our federal government directly created a $40 billion gap between the rich and poor (Brown). Trickle-down economics is a belief in which you help everyone, by helping the rich. Trickle-down economics are ineffective and have only made the poverty problem worse. "Hunger is the direct result of conscious policies of our federal government" (Citizens' 61). The federal government is clearly hurting the hungry more than they are helping. For example, to receive AFDC (Aid to Families with Dependent Children) assistance, families are being forced to separate. You can't be a two-parent family and receive AFDC assistance (Citizens' 59). Families must choose between staying together and getting no aid, or splitting up to get aid. It seems that our government is clearly promoting poor families to separate.

Changes in government policies have made it harder for people to receive any aid at all. Federal budget cuts, and tax changes have taken billions away from the poor. In the Food Stamp Program, the government eliminated the provision of inflation adjustments, and many families were now eliminated from the program altogether (Citizens' 70). Since there is no inflation adjustment, the assistance that is given is worth less. The Food Stamp Program, according to Judith Segal, needs a "more comprehensive program that can immediately give, in addition to a fully adequate diet, any other services to raise standards of living" (75). Children's nutrition programs have also been cut back dramatically. Due to lowering federal subsidies, changing criteria, and alteration of the application process, one million children were dropped off food programs (Citizens' 72). Federal programs were shut down because of technicalities, and many children went hungry. For example, the government shut down a very successful program, the School Lunch and Breakfast Program. Many children depended on those nutritional meals for survival. Allan G. Rodgers, a scholar of federal assistance programs states,

Hunger is no accident either. The policies of denying assistance to many of the neediest people are for the most part the result of deliberate efforts at the federal and state levels to discourage otherwise eligible people from qualifying or staying on public assistance (qtd. in Citizens' 75).

How can a government who says they are for the people, treat their people like this? Our government truly has no concern for the hungry. According to Robert McAdams, "the best techniques . . . cannot overcome the ruinous effects of public policies that shortchange the food supply" (qtd. in Hirchoff, and Kotler xi).

Even though the problems are many, hunger in America can be eliminated. There must be a "national commitment to the proposition that we will not tolerate hunger in our land" (Citizens' 93). There need to be decent paying jobs available, so people can help themselves. The elderly and people who can't work need assistance so "economic distress doesn't bring hunger and malnutrition" (Brown). Children need the School Lunch and Breakfast Program for at least two nutritional meals a day. The Food Stamp Program needs to be changed so people can get nutritional meals. AFDC needs to be changed so families can stay together and still receive aid.

We the public need to express our concern for the hungry through public pressure. We must work to make our political leaders reflect our views in government policies. William Aiken maintains that, "persons have a moral right to be saved from starvation, which is derived from the general right—the right to be saved from preventable death" (Aiken and La Follette 85). That strong statement really opens up your eyes to the true horror of the problem. According to the Citizens' Commission on Hunger in New England, the following steps need to be taken to eliminate hunger in America: Food stamp reform, school nutrition reforms, income supports, and protection of children and the elderly (94).

Before all these steps take place, however, we need to "declare through joint resolution that a National Hunger Crisis exists in America" (Citizens' 94). Once it's recognized that a crisis exists, we can turn our attention toward making sure that hunger never again returns to America (Citizens' 93). There seems to be a serious "lack of commitment" to provide all people with equal basic needs (Segal 2). Most of the public wants solely to blame the government for the hunger problem; people have "ignored their reluctance to dig deeply into their own pockets to eliminate hunger" (Segal 12).

But all of us are hurt when others suffer from hunger—and each of us can make a difference. As Dr. Brown puts it, "Things change when people get involved. . . . Hunger will only be ended when those who do not suffer become as concerned as those who do."

Works Cited

Aiken, William, and Hugh La Follette. World Hunger and Moral Obligation. New Jersey: Prentice-Hall, 1977.

Brown, Larry, Dr. Living Hungry in America. Videocassette. Nassau Community College Cultural Series, 1989. 62 min.

Citizens' Commission on Hunger in New England. American Hunger Crisis: Poverty and Health in New England. Massachusetts: Crane Duplicating, 1984.

Grant, Lee. Down and Out in America. Videocassette. Joseph Feury Productions, Inc., 1985. 57 min.

Hirschoff, Paula M., and Neil Kotler, eds. Completing the Food Chain: Strategies for Combating Hunger and Malnutrition. Washington, D.C.: Smithsonian Institution Press, 1989.

Segal, Judith. Food for the Hungry: The Reluctant Society. Maryland: The John Hopkins Press, 1970.

ALPHABETICAL LIST OF EXERCISES

INDEX

237